D1556925

SPIRITUAL WELL-BEING OF THE ELDERLY

SPIRITUAL WELL-BEING OF THE ELDERLY

Edited By

JAMES A. THORSON, Ed.D.
Director, Gerontology Program
University of Nebraska at Omaha
Omaha, Nebraska

and

THOMAS C. COOK, JR., M.A., M.Div.
Executive Director
National Interfaith Coalition on Aging
Athens, Georgia

CHARLES C THOMAS • PUBLISHER
Springfield • Illinois • U.S.A.

Published and Distributed Throughout the World by

CHARLES C THOMAS • PUBLISHER
Bannerstone House
301-327 East Lawrence Avenue, Springfield, Illinois, U.S.A.

© *1980, by* CHARLES C THOMAS• PUBLISHER
ISBN 0-398-03998-4
Library of Congress Catalog Card Number: 79-21343

*With THOMAS BOOKS careful attention is given to all details of manufacturing
and design. It is the Publisher's desire to present books that are satisfactory as to
their physical qualities and artistic possibilities and appropriate for their
particular use. THOMAS BOOKS will be true to those laws of quality that assure
a good name and good will.*

Printed in the United States of America

OK - 1

Thorson
National Intra-decade Conference on Spiritual Well-being of the Elderly, Atlanta, Ga.,
     1977.
     Spiritual well-being of the elderly.

     Bibliography: p.
     Includes index.
     1. Aged—Religious life—Congresses. 2. Church work with the aged—Congresses.
3. Aged—Psychology—Congresses. I. Thorson, James A., 1946-   II. Cook, Thomas C.
III. Title.
BV4580.N37 1977   230   79-21343
ISBN 0-398-03998-4

080377

To the memory of Virginia Stafford

CONTRIBUTORS

Edith Abraams, M.S., A.C.S.W.
  Social Services Department
  Hebrew Rehabilitation Center for the Aged
  Rosindale, Massachusetts

Shoshana Avner, D.S.W.
  Gerontology Resource Center
  Chicago, Illinois

Constance L. Brennan, M.S.
  Southern Hills Community Mental Health Center
  Jasper, Indiana
  At the time this chapter was written, Ms. Brennan was affiliated
  with the Division of Health Services Administration, Uni-
  versity of Nebraska Medical Center, Omaha.

Philip S. Brown, Th.M., M.A., Executive Director
  Episcopal Home for the Aging
  Southern Pines, North Carolina

Elbert Cole, Th.D., Pastor
  Central United Methodist Church
  Kansas City, Missouri

Rev. Thomas C. Cook, Sr., Minister
  Presbyterian Church in the U.S.
  Laurens, South Carolina

Thomas C. Cook, Jr., M.A., M. Div., Executive Director
  National Interfaith Coalition on Aging
  Athens, Georgia

Msgr. Charles Fahey, M.S.W., Director
All University Gerontological Center
Fordham University
New York, New York
At the time this presentation was made, Monsignor Fahey was
Director of U.S. Catholic Charities, Syracuse, New York.

Roy W. Fairchild, Ph.D., Professor of Education and Social
Psychology
San Francisco Theological Seminary
San Anselmo, California

Arthur Flemming, Ph.D., Chairman
U.S. Civil Rights Commission
Washington, D.C.
At the time this presentation was made, Dr. Flemming was
Commissioner of the U.S. Administration on Aging.

Bruce J. Horacek, Ph.D., Academic Coordinator
Gerontology Program
College of Public Affairs and Community Service
University of Nebraska at Omaha

Carl G. Howie, Ph.D., Minister
First Presbyterian Church
Dearborn, Michigan

Gregory L. Jackson, S.T.M., Pastor
St. Timothy Lutheran Church
Sturgis, Michigan

Robert I. Kahn, D.H.L., Rabbi
Temple Emanu El
Houston, Texas

Martin Luther King, Sr., D. Div., Pastor Emeritus
Ebenezer Baptist Church
Atlanta, Georgia

Margaret E. Kuhn, D.H.L., Convener
The National Gray Panthers
Philadelphia, Pennsylvania

Betty J. Letzig, M.A.
Board of Global Ministries, National Division
United Methodist Church
New York, New York

Mother M. Bernadette deLourdes, O. Carm., A.C.S.W.
Carmelite Sisters for the Aged and Infirm
Trumbull, Connecticut
At the time this presentation was made, Mother Bernadette
was serving as President of the National Council on the Aging.

Paul B. Maves, Ph.D.
Shepherd's Center Training Service
Kansas City, Missouri

Robert W. McClellan, D.Min., Associate Pastor
Point Loma Community Presbyterian Church
San Diego, California

William A. McCreary, M.Div., Pastor
Goode Centennial United Methodist Church
Denver, Colorado

Levi Meier, M.A., M.S., Chaplain
Cedars-Sinai Medical Center
Los Angeles, California
At the time this chapter was written, Rabbi Meier was affiliated
with the Department of Jewish Philosophy, Yeshiva University of Los Angeles.

Stanley V. Michael, Secretary
Benevolences Department
General Council of the Assemblies of God
Springfield, Missouri

Michael B. Miller, M.D., F.A.C.P., Medical Director
  Nathan Miller Center for Nursing Care
  White Plains, New York

Leo Missinne, Ph.D., Professor
  Gerontology Program
  College of Public Affairs and Community Service
  University of Nebraska at Omaha

David O. Moberg, Ph.D., Professor
  Department of Sociology and Anthropology
  Marquette University
  Milwaukee, Wisconsin

Father Daniel M. Munn, D.Min., Associate Professor
  Department of Humanities
  Medical College of Georgia
  Augusta, Georgia

Barbara Pittard Payne, Ph.D., Director
  Gerontology Center
  Georgia State University
  Atlanta, Georgia

Frederick J. Schumacher, S.T.M., D.Min.(Prin.), Pastor
  St. Matthew's Lutheran Church
  White Plains, New York

John W. Stettner, Th.D., Associate Pastor
  Kenilworth Union Church
  Kenilworth, Illinois
  At the time this chapter was written, Dr. Stettner was Professor
  of Pastoral Care, McCormick Theological Seminary, Chicago.

James A. Thorson, Ed.D., Director
  Gerontology Program
  College of Public Affairs and Community Service
  University of Nebraska at Omaha

Ann Vinson, Ph.D.
College of Life-Long Learning
University of Michigan-Wayne State University
Detroit, Michigan

Vicki A. Zoot, R.N., M.H.P.E.
Niles Township Jewish Congregation
Skokie, Illinois

PREFACE

Underlying the uneasiness of many in today's culture is the fear that when individual productivity is curtailed personal worth is diminished. The fear of such a personal "market crash" can set off a variety of destructive emotional and behavioral outcomes that in fact may make an imagined predicament more real.

A sense of personal worth that is independent of one's abililty or position frees aging persons from a panicky fear of the loss of self-worth when economic productivity ceases. The conviction that the worth of self is entrenched in God is fundamental to spiritual well-being.

Institutional religious groups have an inherent mandate to nourish and proclaim such worth. The central credo of the Judeo-Christian traditions, while variously expressed, is the unqualified worth of persons created by God, whatever their status and circumstance. This conviction is the moral energy indispensable to ministry to persons of any age or station. From the standpoint of aging, this conviction is rhetoric unless interpreted in the specificity of individual traditions applied to the lives of older persons in the community. By keeping faith with the structures of faith, the religious sector is in a unique position to contradict the myth that the value of persons is measured primarily by their productivity.

The National Interfaith Coalition on Aging (NICA) has defined spiritual well-being of the elderly as "The affirmation of life in a relationship with God, self, community and environment that nurtures and celebrates wholeness." NICA has further developed the following commentary on the definition:

> The *spiritual* is not one dimension among many in life; rather, it permeates and gives meaning to all life. The term spiritual well-being, therefore, indicates wholeness in contrast to fragmentation and isolation. "Spiritual" connotes our dependence on the source of life, God the creator.
>
> What, then is spiritual well-being? We cannot regard well-being as equated solely with physical, psychological, or social good health. Rather, it is an *affirmation of life*. It is to say "yes" to life in spite of negative circumstances. This is not mere optimism which denies some of

life's realities; rather, it is the acknowledgment of the destiny of life. In the light of that destiny it is the love of one's own life and of the lives of others, together with concern for one's community, society, and the whole of creation, which is the dynamic of spiritual well-being.

A person's affirmation of life is rooted in participating in a community of faith. In such a community one grows to accept the past, to be aware and alive in the present, and to live in hope of fulfillment. Affirmation of life occurs within the context of one's relationship with God, self, community, and environment. God is seen as Supreme Being, creator of life, the source and power that wills well-being. All people are called upon to respond to God in love and obedience. Realizing we are God's children, we grow toward wholeness as individuals, and we are led to affirm our kinship with others in the community of faith as well as the entire human family. Under God and as members of the community of faith, we are responsible for relating the resources of the environment to the well-being of all humanity.

Human wholeness is never fully attained. Throughout life it is a possibility in process of becoming. In the Judeo-Christian tradition(s) life derives its significance through its relationship with God. This relationship awakens and nourishes the process of growth toward wholeness in self, crowns moments of life with meaning, and extols the spiritual fulfillment and unity of the person.

On December 15, 1969, Willis Atwell, then Deputy Commissioner of the U.S. Administration on Aging, convened an ecumenical adhoc group arranged by former Congressman Walter Moeller at the National Lutheran Council Headquarters in New York City. It was here that the term spiritual well-being was first articulated and discussed. The term was used on a test basis when Doctor Grover Hartman, Executive Director of the Indiana Council of Churches, and George Davis of the Indiana Commission on Aging, in collaboration with the Administration on Aging, developed a project to assist churches and synagogues in ministry to older adults in Indiana. The term then found its way into the preparation for the 1971 White House Conference on Aging, chaired by Doctor Arthur S. Flemming and directed by John B. Martin, then Commissioner of the United States Administration on Aging. Doctor David O. Moberg, of the Department of Sociology and Anthropology of Marquette University, working with the Technical Committee, drafted a background paper on spiritual well-being that provided guidance and input into the Section on Spiritual Well-Being of the

1971 White House Conference on Aging. That section reported out a number of recommendations, including one suggesting an intra-decade conference on spiritual well-being of the elderly to be held sometime between the 1971 and 1981 White House Conferences on Aging.

In March of 1972, the National Interfaith Coalition on Aging was born in response to those recommendations of the 1971 White House Conference pertaining to the concerns of the religious sector in meeting the spiritual well-being needs of older Americans. NICA undertook a major project with Older Americans Act funding to provide a nationwide survey of aging programs under religious auspices. During this three-and-one-half-year project, NICA began to examine its own role and to see the need of a working definition of the term *spiritual well-being of the elderly*. Thus, in February of 1975, a consultation representative of major religious traditions and several disciplines convened in Chicago and successfully hammered out a definition and commentary for common use. The definition and commentary, once accepted by the Coalition, provided a foundation for the range and quality of NICA's common task.

As we look at the older persons we serve and whom we will someday become, it is urgent that we provide not just for things— units of service, meals, transportation, and housing—however important these are, but that we make provisions to see that help comes with self-involvement, compassion, dignity, and grace that moves in the direction of wholeness and an affirmation of life that is as important to the provider as to those who are served. To that end, we must use churches and synagogues in every city and town to provide the opportunity for older persons to find personal fulfillment, dignity, and appropriate services given in a supportive setting.

The problem of definition, always demanding of mental and verbal resources, was especially critical because of a wide variety of meanings popularly attached to the term *spiritual* and because of the religious diversities among participating faiths. Nevertheless, not one member of the drafting committee attached less than major importance to that domain represented by the term *spiritual*. Since its adoption in 1975, the definition and commentary have become a reference point, a standard we have used in making application in our respective religious traditions. While the definition was worked out in terms of our concern and understanding of the need, characteristics, and rights of older adults, it is intergenerational in its wording and should be equally useful at any stage of human development from life's beginning to its end.

The National Interfaith Coalition on Aging has grown in its membership to include over thirty religious denominations of Jewish, Roman Catholic, and Protestant traditions. Throughout its existence it has promoted the following objectives that are resonant with the concept and definition of spiritual well-being presented in this book:

> To identify and give priority to those programs and services for the aging that best may be implemented through the resources of the nation's religious sector;

> To vitalize and develop the role of the church and synagogue with respect to their responsibility in improving the quality of life for the aging;

> To stimulate cooperative and coordinated action between the nation's religious sector and national secular, private and public organizations and agencies whose programs and services relate to the welfare and dignity of older persons;

> To encourage the aging to continue giving to society from the wealth of their experiences and to remain active participants in community life.

In the chapters that follow, a variety of approaches are explored in applying the concept of spiritual well-being among differing traditions and disciplines. With a very few exceptions, the chapters have been selected from over seventy presentations given at the 1977 National Intra-decade Conference on Spiritual Well-being of the Elderly, held in Atlanta, Georgia, in fulfillment of the recommendation of the 1971 White House Conference on Aging. Through nationally known speakers, scholars, and practitioners in both religious and gerontological fields, the Conference

developed the four relationships of spiritual well-being identified in the definition, that is, God, self, community, and
environment. The contents of this book have been organized
around the same general outline. Spiritual well-being of the
elderly has thus become not only an issue for the religious sector
but, through the White House Conference on Aging, a concern
for the whole field of secular services for the aging.

Surely, spiritual well-being as a concept must be considered if
we are to be holistic in the involvement of older adults in
American life. David Moberg (1971) has said that spiritual well-
being should be the primary focus of all that is done under
religious auspices:

> If we do not make spiritual well-being our focus, we may sell our
> birthright for a mess of pottage. Which obviously poses certain
> problems, e.g., of the theological and philosophical variation in values
> as to what spiritual well-being is, there is a great need for research just to
> find out what these values are. That is the first step toward determining
> what all of our definitions of spiritual well-being have in common, or
> whether there is such great diversity that we have only spiritual well-
> being according *to each of a variety of traditions.* Since spiritual well-
> being is infused into all the rest of life's activities, experiences, feelings,
> attitudes, beliefs, organizational programs and the like, it is very easy to
> miss its central significance at the very core of human nature. Also, since
> a kind of "spiritual blindness" afflicts people who lack spiritual
> enlightenment, those scientists and scholars who are non-believers in
> God and adopt as an unspoken postulate the denial of the essentially
> spiritual nature of man will refuse to observe evidences of the ontological
> reality of the spiritual component in human nature.

It was a difficult task to select from the more than seventy
presentations the papers that are included in this volume. The
selection process included an assessment by conference evaluators
and the editors of each paper's contribution to the concept of
spiritual well-being and general suitability for publication. In
the end, however, it was the painful job of the editors to select
papers that would work together, as a whole, to enrich the
knowledge base of "spiritual well-being" from a variety of
religious traditions and academic and professional points of
view. A number of outstanding papers from the conference

remain unpublished and are available for inclusion in a future book of readings. It is our hope that these pages and selected papers will encourage those of varying beliefs and disciplines to join in healthy dialogue that will further enrich the spiritual well-being of older Americans and, thereby, improve the quality of life for us all.

Much appreciation must go to Thomas W. Mahler, Director, and the Reverend Jack Ahlers, Program Chairman, and to the following members of the Spiritual Well-being Conference Committee and staff: Brother Joseph Berg, Rev. Earl Kragnes, Lt. Col. Mary E. Verner, Rev. Chenoweth Watson, Ms. Donna McGinty, Mrs. Maretta Carstensen, and Dr. James Thorson.

A debt of thanks is in order to all of our contributors who diligently prepared to share their application of the spiritual well-being definition. Finally, we express appreciation to the Administration on Aging for funding under the Older Americans Act, to the Interreligious Liaison Office of the NRTA/AARP, the University of Georgia Center for Continuing Education, and member denominations without whose contributions and support the event generating these chapters could never have taken place.

THOMAS C. COOK, JR.

REFERENCE

D. O. Moberg, *Spiritual well-being:* Background and issues for the Technical Committee on Spiritual Well-Being, 1971 White House Conference on Aging (Washington, U.S. Government Printing Office, 1971).

CONTENTS

Section III
Spiritual Well-Being in Relation to Self

Contents

Section IV
Spiritual Well-Being in Relation to the Community

Section V
Spiritual Well-Being in Relation to the Environment

Section I
WHAT IS SPIRITUAL WELL-BEING?

Chapter 1

INTRODUCTION

JAMES A. THORSON

This book represents the attempt by many individuals to elaborate on the concept of spiritual well-being as it applies to older adults. Specifically, it provides a variety of perspectives, from various religious traditions and from theoretical and practical points of view, on the central theme of spiritual well-being. Hopefully, the material in this book will stimulate a dialog between persons in the fields of theology and philosophy and their colleagues in the various disciplines related to gerontology.

One of the great frustrations in dealing with this kind of concept is in establishing a clear definition of what exactly spiritual well-being is. The people with whom I have worked on this project have engaged in a great deal of discussion on this topic over the past several years. As a person who comes from the field of gerontology and who has no training in theology, it has often been my observation that the more words added to any particular definition, the less clear and understandable it becomes. A further problem is that we are not aware of a body of data-based research in the area of spiritual well-being. Various highly competent studies can be found in the gerontological literature on attitudes held by and toward the aging, morale studies, and life satisfaction indices. The bulk of this literature has to do with well-being from a social, economic, psychological, or physical point of view; a general, if less than startling, conclusion that can be drawn from them is that—all other things being equal—older people who are well and financially well-off tend to have higher levels of life satisfaction than those who are sick and poor. Somehow this still does not give us an appreciation for the concept that spiritual well-being is of another dimension, over and above physical or economic well-being.

A related problem is the assumption by many that spiritual well-being has a close relationship to religious activities or feelings:

church going, Bible reading, depth of belief, and so on. That is, people who go through the motions one usually associates with being religious are assumed to have high levels of spiritual well-being. This line of thinking usually then gets bogged down in trying to establish measures of religious feeling or intensity, trying to determine if the person who is engaged in many church or synagogue activities has a deeper religious appreciation than the irregular participant. Going further out on this tangent leads to the fascinating question: can an atheist have spiritual well-being? In the words of Jonathan Swift, I will leave this problem to the philosophers.

Such discussion begs what, in my opinion, is a question central to the entire concept: is the person who has spiritual well-being better off because of it? One would assume that the answer to this question is in the affirmative, but there is not a persuasive body of research upon which to draw a conclusion on this issue one way or the other. A danger here is projecting one's own feelings or biases onto the population of older adults. Persons in the community of faith, for example, might naturally assume that because spiritual well-being is important to them personally, it would of course be important to older people in general. On the other hand, some in the field of gerontology who may have no particular religious orientation may not ever consider that matters spiritual may have a great deal of importance to older individuals.

Moberg (1971) advances several well-developed concepts that help to clarify some of these questions. Pointing out that "Belief in God reaches its highest levels and is held with the greatest certainty in the later years of life" (1971, p. 28), Moberg identifies several elements related to the spiritual well-being of the aged. These include sociocultural sources of spiritual needs, relief from anxieties and fears, preparation for death, personality integration, personal dignity, and a philosophy of life. Moberg cites Johnson (1964) in an elaboration of the concept:

> We have seen that the definition of "spiritual" is not so clear and rigidly fixed that it can be separated from the physical, psychological, material, and other aspects of human existence. Instead it is a component or dimension of man which runs through all of the person and his behavior, providing an orientation and focus which pertains to all of the positively valued joys and experiences of living and all of the negative problems and fears of life and death. It provides a basis for coping with

the disruptions of removal (mobility of children and grandchildren, death of spouse and friends, moving away from the old neighborhood), of biological insecurity (illness, death, and disrupted sexual functioning), and of sinfulness with its feelings of guilt. (1971, p. 14)

Another way of arriving at an understanding of spiritual well-being is to describe its absence. I was recently contacted by an attorney from a legal service program who had entered a suit in the local Federal District Court on behalf of an eighty-two-year-old woman who is a resident in a non-profit nursing home (which, incidentally, is operated by a religious order). It seems that she has adapted well to the institution, having lived there for the past seven years. Her personal funds are now exhausted and she will have to be supported by Medicaid. The administration of the nursing home wants her to move somewhere else, because they can only accept a certain percentage of Medicaid patients and stay financially solvent. Since receiving word that she must move, she has become very anxious and her physical condition has deteriorated.

In his case, the attorney argued that since the institution was built in part with Federal funds and loan guarantees, it has some obligation to keep this woman on, even though she no longer has private means and will have to accept Federal support, which will reimburse the home at a lesser rate than is charged private-pay patients. His request of me was to testify that an involuntary transfer would endanger her health. My response was that I had no way to predict whether or not a particular individual would respond negatively to such a transfer. I would, however, be willing to cite examples from the literature (e.g., Frankl, 1963; Blenkner, 1967; Seligman, 1975) that advance persuasive arguments to the effect that people who have all internal control taken away from them, especially in cases of involuntary transfer, are likely to have higher rates of mortality and morbidity. Further, this may be as a result of more than the loss of internal control, but may also be related to the loss of spiritual well-being.

Frankl (1963) details cases of fellow prisoners in the concentration camp who seemed to give up hope and who died shortly thereafter for no physical cause that he could determine. His conclusion was that those who were able to survive the holocaust experience were generally characterized by an inner spiritual strength and will to live. Blenkner (1967) cites several cases of the involuntary transfer of institutionalized populations; the groups' mortality rates invariably were much higher after the transfer than before. Seligman (1975) develops the concept of helplessness, or loss of internal control, and identifies it as a factor in the many cases of unexplained sudden death that he describes: "I suggest that such deaths no longer be seen as unexpected. We should expect that when we remove the vestiges of control over the environment of an already physically weakened human being, we may kill him" (1975, p.186). I would argue that spiritual well-being may well be as important a factor as internal control in survival. It not only has to do with the quality of life, but with the very willingness to live life as well. In short, the person who finds meaning in life will have a reason to live.

One other way to put the idea of spiritual well-being into perspective is by looking at other, closely related concepts. The developmentalists here have given us useful material with which to work. Most readers who have a background in the social sciences are familiar with the developmental stages that have been described by Erikson (1963). One might argue that a state of spiritual well-being parallels Erikson's stage of ego integrity. In a similar manner, those who are familiar with Maslow's (1954) hierarchy may find self-actualization and spiritual well-being to be similar if not exactly the same.

McClusky (1976) has developed a series of stages through which people go that has a particular relevance to late life. McClusky describes a series of needs, from survival, through maintenance, to growth and beyond, that can be arranged into a hierarchy similar to Maslow's in that basic needs must be met before progression to the next can occur. At the most basic level, McClusky identifies *coping needs*, including physical, economic, and educational needs. Second would come *expressive* needs, going beyond survival needs and skills to the concept of sharing oneself with others and the enjoyment of a healthy expression of natural physical capacities. Third is the area of *contributive* needs, including the need to give—the need to be needed. Next in the hierarchy come *influence* needs, the need to shape one's environment and to have an impact within the larger society. The final level described by McClusky deals with the *need for transcendence,* which is related to going beyond the self in order to find meaning in life. Peck (1968) elaborates this concept:

> The constructive way of living the late years might be defined in this way: To live so generously and unselfishly that the prospect of personal death—the night of the ego, it might be called—looks and feels less important than the secure knowledge that one has built for a broader, longer future than any one ego ever could encompass. Through children, through contributions to the culture, through friendships—these are ways in which human beings can achieve enduring significance for their actions which goes beyond the limit of their own skins and their own lives. (1968, p. 91)

To transcend personal considerations, to live life in such a way that physical and economic considerations become unimportant, surely goes beyond simple life satisfaction and begins to describe real spiritual well-being.

The following chapters give a variety of interpretations to spiritual well-being. Some are broad and philosophical, others give a biblical interpretation, and several describe cases or practical applications of spiritual well-being in action. Our hope is that practitioners and scholars in many fields will find meaning in this book and a more complete understanding of the importance of spiritual well-being to the lives of the elderly.

REFERENCES

Blenkner, Margaret. Environmental change and the aging individual. *The Gerontologist,* 1967, 7, 101-105.
Erikson, Erik. *Childhood and society.* New York: W.W. Norton, 1963.
Frankl, Victor. *Man's search for meaning.* New York: Washington Square Press, 1963.
Johnson, Gerald K. Spiritual aspects of aging. *Lutheran Social Welfare Quarterly,* 1964, *4,* 28-36.
Maslow, Abraham. *Motivation and personality.* New York: Harper and Row, 1954.

McClusky, Howard Y. Education for aging: The scope of the field and perspectives for the future. In Stanley Grabowski and W. Dean Mason (Eds.), *Learning for aging.* Washington, D.C.: Adult Education Association of the U.S.A., 1976, 324-355.

Moberg, David O. *Spiritual well-being:* Background and issues for the Technical Committee on Spiritual Well-Being, 1971 White House Conference on Aging. Washington, D.C.: U.S. Government Printing Office, 1971.

Peck, Robert C. Psychological Developments in the Second Half of Life. In Bernice Neugarten (Ed.), *Middle Age and Aging.* Chicago: University of Chicago Press, 1968, 88-92.

Seligman, Martin E.P. *Helplessness.* San Francisco: W.H. Freeman and Company, 1975.

Chapter 2

SPIRITUAL WELL-BEING FROM THE PERSPECTIVE OF THE 1971 WHITE HOUSE CONFERENCE ON AGING

Arthur S. Flemming

The National Interfaith Coalition on Aging is a concrete response to the insights and concerns expressed by the delegates to the second White House Conference on Aging. Those leaders in the religious life of our nation who have responded to that challenge have had a very significant impact on the life of our nation as it confronts the issues that exist in the field of aging. We have been particularly appreciative of what has been done in connection with the development of the report entitled *The Religious Sector Explores Its Mission in Aging.* Our hope is that the processes that have been set in motion as a result of this particular document are processes that will prove to be continuous in the life of our nation. The concluding phrase of the report is striking: "Based upon the data examined in this report and inspection of program description in the NICA data bank, it is the opinion of the present investigator that taken as a whole at present, religious bodies in the United States exhibit a relatively low effort in behalf of the elderly" (Cook, 1976, p. 94).

Of course, there is a good deal of evidence in the report that substantiates that conclusion. There is also a good deal of evidence included in the report that points to some of the reasons for this relatively low effort. For example, in the section dealing with theological education, the survey is able to identify only thirty-seven seminaries in the country that in fact have a true course in gerontology in their curriculum. This means that our theological schools and seminaries are exhibiting the same attitude of neglect toward the field of aging that is exhibited by our other professional schools. Medical schools for the most part have neglected their opportunities in the field of aging.

One of the reasons why local churches and other religious bodies have not had as much of an impact on the field of aging as they might is that we have tended to concentrate too much on the self-centered attitudes that many older persons have. Our mission is to break older persons out of that self-centered attitude, to bring them to the place where they realize that they have just as much of an obligation to serve their fellow human beings as they had at any other stage in life. As the church thinks in terms of its mission to older persons, one of its major responsibilities is to keep underlining the fact that the older person has the obligation to serve others right down to the day of his or her death. Of course, we know from experience that when an older person recognizes and accepts that responsibility it brings a joy and a satisfaction to them that cannot come in any other way.

It is quite clear that the aging person in the United States of America is now to some extent reaping the rewards of an awakened religious community and will undoubtedly in the future reap these rewards to an even greater extent. By fulfilling its spiritual mandate to love God and other people, the religious community at all levels will add the caring, love, and dignity that makes life at all ages beautiful and meaningful.

What are some of the things that should be kept in mind as the religious community endeavors to strengthen its mission to the aged? First we must emphasize the spiritual mandate to love God and other people. We share a common responsibility that we must never pass up an opportunity to help our neighbors to achieve their highest potential. As the church carries forward its mission to all age groups it should seek to obtain converts who are willing to take that commandment, put it in the center of their lives, and act accordingly. To the extent that we succeed in getting persons to renew their committment to that command- ment, we strengthen all programs in the field of aging. The church must never lose sight of this. We have an obligation to see to it that the church as an institution becomes increasingly sensitive to the needs of older persons. We have an obligation and a responsibility to try to place on the conscience of our people their spiritual obligation to visit older persons. When they do, they then become acquainted with the issues that confront the lives of older persons. They begin to identify the desire on the part of older persons not to be put on the shelf but to have the opportunity of continuing to make a significant contribution to life. They become acquainted with the tragedy that confronts those thousands of old persons whose annual income is below the poverty threshold. They begin to confront in a very realistic way the issues that this nation confronts in the area of the delivery of health services to older persons.

When the local church comes into the picture in this way today, it is confronted with opportunities that did not exist a few years ago. We now have fifty state agencies on aging as well as 540 area agencies on aging. We now have over 1,000 nutrition project agencies that are working at the grass roots level. When a visitor comes back to his local church and begins to talk about some of the issues confronting older people, these agencies are a place to turn for help and assistance.

The synagogue and churches within a neighborhood can effectively pool their resources in such a way as to relate in a significant manner to the spiritual needs of older persons. The neighborhood coalition has the opportunity of coming to grips with the relationship of the older person to the family. Twenty-eight percent of the persons 65 and over are living in a home with children. Another thirty-three percent are living within ten minutes of the home of a child; a total of eighty-two percent are living within thirty minutes of the home of one of their children. The extended family is of a different kind than it was fifty years ago. There is a different set of problems in terms of building effective bridges between the children and the older person. What institution in society is better equipped to help build those bridges than the church?

REFERENCES

Cook, Thomas C., Jr. *The religious sector explores its mission in aging.* Athens, Georgia: National Interfaith Coalition on Aging, 1976.

Chapter 3

DELAYED GRATIFICATION AND SPIRITUAL WELL-BEING IN THE ELDERLY

ROY W. FAIRCHILD

A s part of a course in pastoral visitation, near-verbatim reports of conversations with church-oriented people ranging in age from seventy to the mid-eighties have been collected. The central focus of the interviews has been the life review (Butler, 1963), but time-perspectives and goal-orientations were included as well. In some cases an unexpected phenomenon was encountered: a delayed gratification pattern of behavior that, at first glance, seemed strangely obsolete for persons of advanced age. The limited sample permits no estimate of the proportion of older people manifesting this pattern of behavior. This chapter is a first attempt to identify constructs that might help to understand these findings, constructs that could be later tested. The chapter will also indicate the relevance of these constructs to the emerging concept of spiritual well-being.

Basic to the concepts of "will power," "self-control," and "ego-strength" is the ability to postpone immediate gratification for the sake of future consequences, to impose delays of reward upon oneself, and to tolerate this self-initiated frustration for the sake of valuable but deferred outcomes. Reviews of many of the studies of delayed gratification have been published by Fairchild (1971) and Mischel (1974).

Primary socialization in most active religious families includes an emphasis on the delay of gratification. Most variants of the Judeo-Christian tradition teach the desirability of "time binding" (Sarbin, 1954), that is, acting in the present although the justification for so acting will not take place until some time in the future. This emphasis on the future gratification of desires (especially pleasure-seeking, sexual, and aggressive impulses) is ordinarily considered in these traditions as related to spiritual

12

well-being. It is frequently encountered in religious homes in such sayings as "duty before pleasure" or "beans before dessert."

It is difficult to conceive of socialization or even civilization without the ability to delay some impulses; complex goal-directed behavior depends on this capacity. However, in an earlier review of the research (Fairchild, 1971), it was contended that it is possible to construct criteria that differentiate growth-inhibiting from adaptive forms of delayed gratification and their significance for mental health. Several brief cases that relate to this question follow:

Case #1

A student made a call on behalf of her congregation on Mrs. W., a widow 80 years of age whom she knew slightly. She was known as an immaculate housekeeper. The student reports: "It was one of those beautiful, long, lavender spring evenings when the scent of wisteria and the fading twilight made everything else seem extraneous. Mrs. W. met me at the door in her apron and dustcap and we chatted there for a few minutes; she did not invite me in, saying her house was not in order. I called her attention to the sunset and the scent and invited her to come outside and take it in. She said, no, she couldn't. She was about to wax her hall floor. This was her floor-cleaning day. She had been working since 8 A.M. and still had mountains of work to do. She lived by herself, and according to our impressions, seldom invited anyone into her home. So, few would see the crystaline perfection of her floors, the glistening furniture, and the sterile toilet bowl."

Case #2

Mr. M., aged 85 and a widower, according to his son not very adept at providing himself meals in his own home, asked to discuss the Meals on Wheels program with the church worker. After communicating the information, she mentioned the fee. Immediately Mr. M. commented with some heat he could not afford it and requested a lower rate than the $2.00 a day service charge. The worker learned that Mr. M. was receiving $475 a month from investments as well as a Social Security check for $120. His monthly expenses did not exceed $300. Mr. M. claimed he needed his money for "a rainy day" and for his old age and withdrew his application in spite of the worker's effort to show him it would be no strain on his budget.

These two cases, and many others like them, would appear to be examples of the "obligatory repetition" pattern and perceptual distortion of present resources that Kubie (1974) has identified as a neurotic process. Other hypotheses, however, are possible.

In contrast to these two cases, other people of the same age range were encountered who clearly were working in the present for goals in their personal future, sometimes at considerable sacrifice.

Case #3

> A former doctoral student reported that one of the older persons (late seventies) in his church program had become, in his retirement, an avid nurseryman, a leader in the development of hybrid camelias. When asked about his eager present involvement in raising camelia plants from seeds, a process requiring much patience and meticulous care, he replied, "We camelia growers have a saying: 'May you not live to see the blossoms from the last camelia seed you plant.'"

Charlotte Bühler's autobiographical studies (1968) indicate that for many older adults life continues to be a challenging project involving self-determination toward long-range goals. How are we to understand the differences in these two orientations toward delayed gratification? Do they have implications for the concept of spiritual well-being?

The external demographic variables that seem to be related to the ability to delay gratification have been reviewed earlier (Fairchild, 1971). It may be productive now to explore some aspects of "interiority," the intrapsychic process that Neugarten claims as a potentially more fruitful realm for the study of major changes in aging populations (1966). Two constructs that need much deeper exploration for the subject at hand and for the concept of spiritual well-being are the *self-concept* and the *perception of a personal future*. In self-concept investigation, the sense of a persisting personal identity and the sense of personal worth or control would seem to be two important components. We know little, if anything, empirically about the influence of religious beliefs and values on the self-concept, even though Moberg (1965, 1968) has demonstrated that deeply held traditional Christian beliefs and church participation are related to a good personal adjustment in old age. The second construct is the perception of a personal future with its closely related sense of hope and its relationship to projected life span, time-dimension focus, and perspectives on death.

With few exceptions, as Wylie (1961) and Gergen (1971) have pointed out, most studies of the self-concept have been deficient in analytic rigor. The term is often used synonymously with self-image, self-esteem, identity, and ego-strength. It is not clear how the consistency or inconsistency of the self-concept across the life span contributes either to psychosocial adaptation or to spiritual well-being. Lecky (1969), in his advocacy of consistency theory, contrasts sharply with Lifton's (1969) idea that the best adapted and healthiest people at our time and place in history have "protean" self-images that are constantly changing.

According to Lifton's view (1969), the "dated" self-concepts found in Cases #1 and #2 would be considered maladaptive, since they seem to have been defined in terms of "the frozen crystaline structures of the past." In Neugarten's framework (1964), the house-cleaner and frugal ex-businessman would be placed in the "constricted-defended" group of aging persons, in contrast to the camelia grower, who is open to the future and "integrated." Lowenthal (1977) advances the intriguing suggestion that a former self might be the main reference for many of the elderly. Bengston (1973) has suggested that this is the middle-aged self. This may be the self they endeavor to protect through reminiscence and life reviewing, since middle-age might be the time of the greatest remembered worth and independence. Landis's (1970) concept of ego-boundaries also sheds light on the "dated" delayed gratification behavior we have encountered. Landis suggests that inner boundaries between the past and present self become loose and diffuse to compensate for an increase in the impermeability of boundaries between the present self and others. With increasing socal isolation, the future is muted, and the time orientation is focused more on the past in older people. By implication, where there is a firm perception of the difference of past and present by a self-in-process-of-becoming, and which is open to new experiences with others, we would expect a present and future focus. Case #3 may fall into this description. Paradoxically, the delayed gratification pattern of behavior in the first two cases referred to the past, not to the future.

This brings us now to our second proposed construct, the *perception of a personal future*. It is assumed that everyone, at any stage of adulthood, experiences St. Augustine's three presents: "a present of things past, a present of things present, a present of things future." Obviously, these presents assume different ratios in individual lives, and at different stages of the life cycle, and in relation to different conditions of mental health. Morale in older people is associated with a future orientation, rather than past. The study of 435 elderly people by Pierce and Clark (1973) identified three factors associated with good morale: being able to look at one's whole life with a predominant sense of satisfaction and perhaps accomplishment; an unruffled and low-stress approach to present day-to-day living; and a sense of anticipation and will to live for the future. These findings would seem to bear out Carl Jung's clinical observation of almost five decades ago:

> For many people too much unlived life remains over. Sometimes (these are) potentialities which they could never have lived with the best of wills, so that they approach the threshold of old age with unsatisfied demands which inevitably turn glances backward... For them a prospect and a goal is absolutely necessary. That is why all great religions hold out the promise of a life beyond, of a supermundane goal which makes it possible for mortal man to live in the second half of life with as much purpose and aim as the first. (1931)

This observation is consistent with Chiriboga's significant study of time and the life course, based on 216 men and women undergoing normative transitions (1973). Among older respondents, most of those with high morale were not concerned with "working over" the past in reminiscence; they were hopeful and oriented to the future. Furthermore, those with a future-time orientation were more likely to expect to die at a later date than were those who were past-oriented. Future-oriented older people were judged as of greater psychological competence (whereas future-oriented younger respondents were more apt to be rated incompetent).

Marjorie Fiske Lowenthal, in a personal communication with the author, advances the very suggestive hypothesis that those elderly who focus on the present or past and give up future goals are those who have become more self-protective, stress-avoidant, or hedonistic as they age. In contrast, those who have a history of strong commitment to goals may focus on the present without losing their drive toward future goals.

Death-awareness is a part of the aging process. How does the religiously oriented person confront death as part of his or her future? Until recently, findings have been contradictory on this question. For example, Swenson (1961) and Jeffers (1961) found more fearful reactions to prospective death among those with little if any religious orientation. On the other hand, studies by Feifel (1956) found religious persons more afraid of dying than non-religious persons. The conflict in such findings is probably due to the practice of adopting gross, behavioral measures of religiosity (for example, church participation) and failing to discern different qualities of religious faith that might account for differential responses. In a recently published study, Spilka and his associates (1977), using psychometric approaches to measure the now familiar categories of "intrinsic-committed" religiousness and "extrinsic-consensual" religiousness first suggested by Gordon Allport (1967), found much *less* death anxiety among those who held their faith in an "intrinsic-committed" fashion (open, flexible, internalized) than those whose faith commitment was judged "extrinsic" and based on instrumental and utilitarian motives. The former, with lower death anxiety, tended to hold more positive death perspectives. That is, they saw death in terms of "courage" (an opportunity to show strength and to realize their highest values), and an "afterlife-as-reward" orientation (death leads to a benevolent eternity). Thus for the "intrinsically" religious any delay of gratification is seen as being perceived to have a final pay-off in terms of spiritual well-being.

REFERENCES

Allport, G.W. Personal religious orientation and prejudice. *Journal of Personality and Social Psychology*, 1967, *5*, 432-443.

Bengston, V.C. *The social psychology of aging.* Indianapolis: Bobbs-Merrill, 1973.

Bühler, C., & Massarik, E. *The course of human life.* New York: Springer Publishing Co., 1968.

Butler, R.N. The life review: An interpretation of reminiscence in the aged. *Psychiatry*, 1963, *26*, 65-76.

Chiriboga, D.A. Time and the life course (Unpublished manuscript), 1973.

Fairchild, R.W. Delayed gratification: A psychological and religious analysis. In M. Strommen (Ed.), *Research on religious development.* New York: Hawthorne Books, 1971, 156-210.

Feifel, H. Older persons look at death. *Geriatrics*, 1956, *11*, 127-130.

Gergen, K.J. *The concept of self.* New York: Holt, Rinehart and Winston, 1971.

Jeffers, F.C., Nichols, C.R., & Eisdorfer, C. Attitudes of older people toward death. *Journal of Gerontology*, 1961, *16*, 53-56.

Jung, C.G. The stages of life. In *Collected works*, Vol. 8 (1931). Princeton, New Jersey: Princeton University Press, 1969, 387-403.

Kubie, L.S. The nature of the neurotic process. In S. Arieti (Ed.), *American handbook of psychiatry*, Vol. 3. New York: Basic Books, 1974, 3-16.

Landis, B. Ego boundaries. *Psychological issues*, Monograph 24, Vol. 6. New York: International Universities Press, 1970.

Lecky, P. *Self consistency: A theory of personality.* Garden City, New York: Anchor Press, 1969.

Lifton, R.J. *Boundaries: Psychological man in revolution.* New York: Vintage Books, 1969.

Lowenthal, M.F. Toward a sociopsychological theory of change in adulthood and old age. In J. Birren & W. Schaie (Eds.), *Handbook of the psychology of aging.* New York: Van Nostrand, 1977.

Mischel, W. Process in delay of gratification. In *Advances in experimental social psychology*, Vol. 7. New York: Academic Press, 1974, 249-292.

Moberg, D.O. Christian beliefs and personal adjustment in old age. *Journal of the American Scientific Affiliation*, 1968, *10*, 8-12.

Moberg, D.O. Religiosity in old age. In B. Neugarten (Ed.), *Middle age and aging.* Chicago: University of Chicago Press, 1968, 497-508.

Moberg, D.O., & Taves, M.J. Church participation and adjustment in old age. In Rose, A., & Peterson, W. (Eds.), *Older people and their social world.* Philadelphia: F.A. Davis Co., 1965.

Neugarten, B. (Ed.). *Personality in middle and late life.* New York: Atherton Press, 1964.

Neugarten, B. Adult personality: A developmental view. *Human Development*, 1966, *9*, 61-73.

Pierce, R.C., & Clark, M. Measurement of morale in the elderly. *International Journal of Aging and Human Development*, 1973, *4*, 83-101.

Sarbin, R.T. Role theory. In Z. Lindsey (Ed.), *Handbook of social psychology*. Cambridge, Massachusetts: Addison-Wesley, 1954, 221-258.

Spilka, B., *et al.* Death and personal faith: A psychometric investigation. *Journal for the Scientific Study of Religion*, 1977, *16*, 169-178.

Swenson, W.M. Attitudes toward death in an aged population. *Journal of Gerontology*, 1961, *16*, 49-52.

Wylie, R.C. *The self concept: A critical survey of research literature*. Lincoln: University of Nebraska Press, 1961.

Chapter 4

SOCIAL INDICATORS OF SPIRITUAL WELL-BEING

David O. Moberg

Precisely a decade ago, at the first research conference of the Rossmoore-Cortese Institute for the Study of Retirement and Aging of the University of Southern California, a conclusion was drawn from a summary of research findings on religion and aging. It was indicated that besides the five dimensions of religiosity identified by Glock (1962) there may be "a *spiritual* component of religiosity which pertains rather directly to man's relationships to God and which cuts across or infuses all the other dimensions" (Moberg, 1967c, p. 42). In spite of its transcendent nature, it was encouraged that this spiritual component be given consideration in scientific research:

> Possibly future developments in behavioral science theory and methodology will bring the analysis of this central element of Judeo-Christian religion into the sphere of the social sciences. If so, our sciences will significantly expand, and we will discover principles of religious development that will make significant practical as well as theoretical contributions to all of the professions that are concerned with the welfare of the aging. (pp. 42-43)

Today we are on the verge of a quantum leap forward toward the fulfillment of that visionary dream. This chapter summarizes some of the developments that suggest that spiritual well-being is becoming a part of social and behavioral science research. Our intent is not to survey the steadily expanding literature related to the subject, but rather to call attention to some of the research developments, together with accompanying problems and tentative findings, in which we are personally involved.

20

Social Indicators and the Quality of Life

A parallel trend during the past decade has been rapid growth of the social indicators movement. Stimulated by demands for evaluation, monitoring, social accounting, and especially by a reaction against overreliance upon monetary values as in the case of economic indicators, it has moved toward the development of regular and systematic measures of the health of the nation and its various subdivisions. Focusing upon challenges to policy and needs for social planning, it has included indicators of the population's health and illness, social mobility, income, poverty levels, crime and delinquency, public order and safety, learning, physical environment, art, science, social participation, alienation, and other conditions. One of its most significant documents, a government report entitled *Toward a Social Report,* includes the following definition:

> A social indicator ... may be defined to be a statistic of direct normative interest which facilitates concise comprehensive and balanced judgments about the condition of major aspects of a society. It is in all cases a direct measure of welfare and is subject to the interpretation that, if it changes in the "right" direction, while other things remain equal, things have gotten better, or people are "better off." (U.S. Department of Health, Education, and Welfare, 1969, p. 97)

Many social indicators are multidimensional indexes that summarize a combination of data from two or more single statistics (see, e.g., Krendel, 1971).

An important subsidiary trend within the social indicators movement has been the development of Quality of Life (QOL) measures of the social well-being of people. Both objective and subjective measures have been included among the QOL indicators (Smith, 1973; Campbell *et al.*, 1976); these studies concluded that religious faith was an important domain of personal resources, in spite of the researchers' admission that they invested only cursory attention to the religious domain.

At least seven interrelated factors contribute to the relative neglect or complete omission of religious variables in the social indicators and QOL movement (Moberg and Brusek, 1977).

These are the religious liberty and church-state separation provisions of the U.S. Constitution, the orientation of most studies toward public policy, the dearth of federal research funds for studies dealing explicitly and directly with religion, the lack of measuring instruments of religion in relationship to quality of life, philosophical and theological assumptions and values that subtly influence the research agenda, the absence of operational distinctions and definitional clarity in the use of relevant concepts, and the lack of consensus about the basic definition of QOL itself.

The net effect of the omission or slighting of religious variables reinforces the impression that religion is irrelevant to the subject. A vicious cycle of self-perpetuating neglect of religious indicators is evident in the QOL movement. The philosophical-religious values of scientists intrude much more readily in it than in many other areas of investigation, limiting the choice and scope of variables and reflecting theoretical and methodological paradigms that are only marginally relevant to the problem at hand.

These problems can be overcome by focusing upon spiritual well-being instead of religion and by developing indicators of spiritual health and illness that can be used in the context of social and behavioral science research. Although explicit exploratory work toward that goal has only recently been initiated, earlier research on religion and personal adjustment in old age (Moberg, 1951, 1967a, 1967b, 1971, 1974, 1975) can be interpreted in retrospect as stepping stones toward the objective of bringing spiritual well-being into the quality of life movement. These publications summarize the findings of relevant studies on various aspects of religion in the later years, provide a theoretical foundation for research on the spiritual nature of man, indicate that such inquiry should be as feasible as that on numerous other topics not susceptible to direct empirical investigation (e.g., intelligence, motivation, authoritarianism, values, pain, anomie, alienation, attitudes, and sentiments), and call for empirical investigations of spiritual health and illness. Rather than recapitulating what is in those published resources, the progress of more recent research will be summarized.

Exploratory Research with Students

During the spring semester of 1975-76, this author taught Marquette University's Practicum in Sociology, a course designed to give senior sociology majors experience in the application of sociological research methods and theory to the investigation of a selected problem. Together with two graduate students, the eleven men and women who completed the course conducted exploratory research on spiritual well-being leading toward the ultimate goal of building an instrument for the measurement of spiritual health and illness. In addition to writing a paper on the perspectives of an assigned sociological theorist toward topics related to spiritual well-being, each student wrote a critique of the NICA (1975) definition of spiritual well-being and other briefer reports, interviewed several persons about spiritual well-being, and helped to construct a pretest draft of an exploratory questionnaire.

The NICA (1975) definition, "Spiritual Well-Being is the affirmation of life in a relationship with God, self, community and environment that nurtures and celebrates wholeness," was presented as a working tool for the research at the beginning of the semester. Even with the help of the supporting commentary, however, the students found the definition impossible to use as a guide to empirical research. (Of course, it was not written for that purpose.) The greatest difficulty resides in the vagueness or non-operational nature of basic concepts like *affirmation, relationship, nurtures, celebrates,* and *wholeness* used in the definition. The phenomenological and existential orientation of the definition makes it so subjective that it cannot be used for the relatively objective kinds of investigation generally favored in sociological surveys. As a result, it is impossible to develop testable hypotheses, gather pertinent data, analyze them, and then determine whether to accept or reject the hypotheses. Except for "participating in a community of faith," behavioral indicators of spiritual well-being are very difficult to develop on the basis of the NICA definition, and even that one is viewed as a means to the end of affirming life, rather than directly as an end in itself. The class did not attempt to develop attitudinal statements out of the

definition and its commentary as a basis for questions addressed
to individuals about their own inner spiritual experiences,
feelings, and beliefs but instead proceeded to interview friends,
acquaintances, professional persons, and strangers in an effort to
discover people's conceptions about the nature of spiritual well-
being. The interviews were facilitated by reviewing the experiences of Edwards *et al.* (1974) in their case studies and
interpretations of the definition of "spiritual maturity," an
analogous but not synonymous concept, by attending and
critiquing a symposium on "Empiricism, Values, and Spiritual
Development" sponsored by Marquette's College of Education
and by weekly sharing of experiences and problems.

Initially the interviews were completely unstructured, each
student drawing out respondents in his or her own way. Students
were encouraged to let the interview take a natural course but to
be sure to cover a broad range of questions at some point in the
structured conversation. By the end of February the reported
interviews revealed numerous components in the understandings
of people when confronted with the concept of "spiritual well-
being." They included the following:

Mental-emotional states

Psychological well-being
Stablility in one's spirit
A state enabling one to do his or her best and accept what one
   cannot understand
A state of mind in people who are relatively free of oppression
Not worrying

Feelings

A feeling of tranquility or inner peace
A feeling that the universe will treat one right
Feeling good about oneself and other people
Feeling happy with oneself or content
Optimism—looking at this world as a great place
Being prosperous and happy with oneself

Happiness with life on earth and with how one feels toward
other people
Peace of mind and ability to extend it outwardly toward others
Being comfortable religiously
An inner feeling that you are at peace with Christ and fellow
people

Relationships and reality-orientation

How one relates to environment, friends, and religion
Good contact with reality
Loving oneself and the world around oneself
Recognition of one's interdependence with other people
Ability to admit the need for other people

Meaning, destiny, goal attainment

Achievement of physical and mental goals
Knowing where one is going in life
A world view of what is in store for you; a worthwhile destiny
Meaning to life
Ability to face death
Working toward a goal
Inner happiness and security from a sense of personal ful-
fillment in life
Belief in the hereafter and need to work to gain the goal of
enjoying that feeling
Search for the good life

Autonomy

Being able to live your own life; being comfortable because
you are in control

Religious faith

Peace with God
Peace of mind in relationship to God

Being a Christian
Ultimate harmony within the soul and for all that the soul
 depends upon (religious; eternal)
Belief in God and all He does to help His people
Being content with God; some sort of connection with Him
A personal relationship with God
Loving, devotional reliance upon God
A state in which you live in God's love, which is our
 spiritual life source
Something given by God, but not to everyone—to the lucky
 few; a gift of love, happiness
Being happy with yourself and believing in a Supreme Being
Faith in the existence of an ultimate plan for the universe
 through Jesus Christ

The diversity of the list is so great that it is obvious that most
people interviewed were unable to call up a societally developed
stereotype of "spiritual well-being." The concept is not a part of
everyday communication.

One of the interesting observations was that most persons
interviewed who were from the helping professions of medicine,
social work, and psychotherapy were confused and vague about
the nature of spiritual health. That may be a simple consequence
of the haphazard selection of interviewees, but it suggests the
desirability of making a systematic study of such people.

Later in the semester an interviewing guide was developed as a
means toward improving the quality and comparability of the
interviews. Its four main topics were the definition of spiritual
well-being, indicators thereof, its causes, sources, and facilitators,
and its consequences. Each of these was elaborated by ten to
fifteen subtopics and questions.

Based upon the interviews and other perspectives gained
throughout the semester, a pretest draft of a questionnaire for the
exploratory study of spiritual well-being was developed. Its
seventy items included opinions about spiritual well-being,
characteristics of spiritual health, influences upon the respon-
dent's own spiritual well-being, evaluators of spiritual well-
being, and background information. It was individually admin-

istered to persons selected by the students in the practicum and to small group of sociology majors on a liberal arts college campus. A total of eighty-two persons responded—thirty-nine males, forty-two females, and one who failed to identify gender. Only five were aged fifty and over; six were between twenty-five and forty-nine, and the other seventy-one were aged twenty-four or younger. The questionnaire and distribution of responses appears as an appendix to this chapter. It is not possible to generalize to any particular group of people on the basis of the findings because the sample was selected haphazardly, not in any systematic manner. Nevertheless, the response patterns suggest some interesting topics for further study. For example, although these respondents generally believe that everybody, or at least most people, can have spiritual well-being, they also felt that the majority do not have it.

Several impressions emerged from this exploratory study. First, there is substantial overlap between the concepts and indicators related to spiritual well-being and those relevant to good mental health. Second, considerable conceptual vagueness and definitional confusion surrounds the notion of spiritual health, even among college students and people in the helping professions. Third, the criterion problem is one of the most significant issues for research. These observations contributed to the next stage of investigation.

Validity: The Criterion Issue

One of the most complex problems in research aimed at developing social indicators of spiritual well-being pertains to the question of validity. In order to differentiate between spiritual well-being or health and spiritual illness it is necessary to make value judgments. Because the spiritual has been related more frequently to religious institutions than to any of the others, it is likely that they will be the primary source of the criteria used to define the concept and to determine which specific observable phenomena may be used as its indicators. Several possibilities can be suggested.

It is possible in our pluralistic society that no single set of criteria can be developed that will be satisfactory to all groups. As a result, each major religious and ideological school of thought may establish its own criteria as to what constitutes wholesome patterns of spiritual life. Reflecting the diversity evident even between denominational branches of major religious families, these may diverge on many levels of belief, religious practices, actions considered right and wrong, and other topics. If so, what is considered "healthy" by one group could be defined as "sick" or "heretical" by another. The consequence for social and behavioral scientists would be the necessity to construct as many instruments for the measurement of spiritual well-being as there are value-domains.

A second possibility is that even in the midst of such diversity, there is a common central core of indicators upon which all agree, regardless of the scope and nature of disagreements about other topics. If that should be the case, an instrument, or set of instruments, could be constructed to "measure" the common core, and they could be supplemented by special modules or tests for the criteria about which there is disagreement.

A third possibility is that the broad range of differences so evident on the surface will prove to be illusory when efforts are made to develop objective indicators. Perhaps diverse religious values are reflected in similar behavior and attitudes. If so, the same instrument could serve all ideological camps, with only the terminology, interpretations, and applications adjusted to fit the uniqueness of each respective group.

Only extensive, painstaking research can determine which of these possibilities prevails. In any event, mere opinion gathering from the general population will hardly serve as a satisfactory foundation for determining which indicators reflect spiritual health and illness. This issue cannot be settled by taking a popular vote, nor even by gleaning a consensus from the frequent reference to the word "spiritual" and its derivations in the popular press.

What is considered spiritually healthy reflects a value orientation that, in the final analysis, rests upon a faith commitment. Typically, that commitment is so interiorized that it is not evident even to professional persons who hold it, sometimes with the belief that they are completely objective, without realizing the postulates and assumptions unconsciously hidden in the depths of their being. Revealing their commitments to a theoretical paradigm or other normative source and subjecting them to rational examination can help to promote investigations that will ground the concept of spiritual health normatively, theoretically, experientially, empirically, methodologically, and semantically.

It is likely that the most beneficial research will progress simultaneously within several ideological frames of reference. Research has been started interviewing evangelical Christians to discover the criteria, definitions, and observable indicators they implicitly use in diagnosing spiritual health and illness. Pat Brusek, research assistant at Marquette University, is interviewing Roman Catholic priests, members of religious orders, and other religious leaders for the same purpose. It is hoped that others will do similar work in Orthodox and Reform Judaism, liberal Protestantism, Islam, Hinduism, Marxism, and other ideological and theological contexts. By cross-checking with each other, the dialogue and interchange will have a refining and correcting influence upon the conclusions tentatively reached at each stage of the research efforts to develop social indicators of spiritual well-being in the quality of life movement. Constructive criticism and comparative analysis will contribute significantly to the development of this complex subject.

Major strides toward that goal are in preparation. At the annual meeting of the Association for the Sociology of Religion in Chicago in September of 1977, approximately a dozen papers were presented in two sessions devoted to research reports and theoretical studies on spiritual well-being. The Ninth World Congress of Sociology in Uppsala, Sweden, in 1978 included a section on spiritual well-being as part of the Sociology of Religion Research Committee's program at which another dozen papers from almost as many nations were presented. Added to the papers of the 1977 NICA Conference, they make a substantial contribution to the refinement of the definition of spiritual well-being and the development of appropriate social indicators for theoretical and applied research in the social and behavioral sciences.

If similar progress is made in psychology, theology, religious education, history, philosophy, anthropology, and the other academic disciplines relevant to spiritual well-being, and if parallel headway is made in the helping professions, synagogues, and churches, we shall be much better able to help our aging population at all ages to fill their time with "mental and spiritual adventures" (Carrel, 1939, p. 186) and thus to enhance instead of diminish their spiritual well-being.

APPENDIX

Pretest Draft
Exploratory Study on Spiritual Well-Being

Our exploratory study on the topic of spiritual well-being has revealed a wide range of ideas about that subject. We want to have your opinions and help.

Please answer each of these questions by checking the answer that is correct or that is closest to your *personal opinion*. If you wish to add comments or qualifications, you may do so in the margins or by adding as many sheets of comments as you wish.

You personally will not be identified, so your answers will be confidential. Summaries of the results from you and many other people will be useful in the research and may be shared in future publications.

Note: Wherever you see the initials SWB they refer to "spiritual well-being" or to "spiritual health."

(Responses are indicated on the questionnaire for the present sample)

Opinions about Spiritual Well-Being (SWB)

For each of the following items, check SA if you *strongly agree*, A if you *agree*, TA if you *tend to agree*, TD if you *tend to disagree*, D if you *disagree*, and SD if you *strongly disagree*. (NR=no response)

1. It is possible for a person to know whether he or she has SWB. SA 23, A 33, TA 22, TD 4, D 0, SD 0.

2. It is possible for people to know whether someone else has SWB. SA 7, A 20, TA 23, TD 22, D 8, SD 2.

3. People are more likely to believe advice from persons who have SWB than from other people. SA 11, A 21, TA 18, TD 18, D 11, SD 2, NR 1.

4. Having SWB gives meaning to life. SA 31, A 27, TA 4, D 0, SD 1, NR 1.

5. SWB helps people make decisions. SA 21, A 35, TA 19, TD 6, D 0, SD 0, NR 1.

6. SWB has no effect at all upon decision-making. SA 3, A 3, TA 3, TD 22, D 28, SD 22, NR 1.

7. People who are sick (physically ill) are likely also to be spiritually ill. SA 2, A 3, TA 10, TD 16 D 27, SD 24.

8. Rich people are more likely to have SWB than poor people. SA 1, A 5, TA 3, TD 19, D 15, SD 39.

9. SWB is a condition which one either has or does not have. SA 6, A 14, TA 19, TD 21, D 10, SD 7, NR 4.

10. SWB is something one can have and then lose. SA 11, A 31, TA 23, TD 5, D 6, SD 6.

11. SWB is a process of growth and development. SA 28, A 40, TA 9, TD 11, D 4, SD 0.

12. Some people have more SWB than others do. SA 26, A 34, TA 11, TD 6, D 3, SD 2.

13. Most of the time an organized religion (church, synagogue,

temple, etc.) hinders SWB more often than it helps it.
SA _5_, A _11_, TA _9_, TD _23_, D _30_, SD _2_.

14. How many people can have SWB? Everybody _64_, Most people _14_, About half _0_, A few people _2_, Nobody _1_. NR _1_

15. How many people *do* have SWB? Everybody _5_, Most people _17_, About half _16_, A few people _31_, Nobody _2_. Not sure _1_, NR _10_

16. In which period of life is a person most likely to have SWB? Childhood _3_, Teen-age (adolescence) _4_, Young adulthood _11_, Middle age _12_, Old age _22_, All are equal _20_, NR _2_

18. Does (or did) your mother have SWB? Yes _51_, No _8_, Not sure _20_, Don't know _3_.

19. Does (or did) your father have SWB? Yes _44_, No _6_, Not sure _25_, Don't know _7_.

Characteristics of Spiritual Health

Indicate whether each of the following items is essential (E) to having SWB, most likely to be present (P) if one has SWB, most likely to be absent (A), or not related at all (NR) to spiritual well-being.

20. Happiness: E _29_, P _47_, A _2_, NR _4_.
21. Being successful: E _5_, P _31_, A _6_, NR _39_.
22. Peace with God: E _52_, P _18_, A _3_, NR _7_.
23. Good physical health: E _9_, P _28_, A _6_, NR _38_.
24. Inner peace: E _59_, P _18_, A _1_, NR _3_.
25. Being good to others: E _25_, P _50_, A _1_, NR _6_.
26. Finding meaning in life: E _44_, P _32_, A _4_, NR _2_.
27. Faith in Christ: E _31_, P _28_, A _3_, NR _19_.
28. Faith in people: E _26_, P _50_, A _1_, NR _5_.
29. Helping others: E _22_, P _49_, A _3_, NR _8_.

30.   Harmony with oneself: E 64,   P 14,   A 2, NR 2.
31.   Good morals: E 25,   P 40,   A 6, NR 9.
32.   Having many friends: E 7,   P 28,   A 6, NR 40.

Influences on Spiritual Well-Being

Please check whether each of the following affects or has affected *your own* SWB very much (VM), much (M), some (S), a little (L), or not at all (N).

33.   School or college: VM 16,   M 24, S 22,   L 11,   N 9.
34.   Government: VM 3,   M 4,   S 13,   L 28,   N 33.
35.   Church: VM 25,   M 13,   S 22,   L 28,   N 10.
36.   Newspapers: VM 1,   M 6,   S 24,   L 18,   N 33.
37.   Television: VM 3,   M 4,   S 22,   L 20,   N 33.
38.   Radio: VM 3,   M 5,   S 21,   L 25,   N 28.
39.   A social club: VM 4,   M 16,   S 26,   L 14,   N 22.
40.   Friends: VM 27,   M 29,   S 15,   L 7,   N 4.
41.   Family: VM 38,   M 29,   S 7,   L 3,   N 3.
42.   Clergy: VM 21,   M 16,   S 22,   L 9,   N 14.
43.   God or a Supreme Being: VM 46, M 18,   S 9,   L 4, N 4.
44.   Angels: VM 4,   M 3,   S 7,   L 14,   N 54.
45.   Demons or evil spirits: VM 5,   M 3,   S 12,   L 12, N 50.
46.   Your astrological sign and horoscope: VM 2,   M 2, S 2,   L 3,   N 72.
47.   Having a good occupation or job: VM 6,   M 16, S 23,   L 12,   N 25.
48.   Money in a bank or savings and loan association: VM 5, M 7,   S 16,   L 14,   N 39.

49. Hard work: VM 12, M 24, S 25, L 8, N 13.

50. Attending church: VM 14, M 14, S 19, L 13, N 22.

51. Praying: VM 23, M 19, S 20, L 8, N 12.

52. Bible reading: VM 13, M 6, S 21, L 17, N 25.

53. Holy Communion: VM 15, M 13, S 21, L 16, N 16.

54. Personal crisis like illness: VM 16, M 22, S 19,
  L 10, N 15.

55. Death of a family member or friend: VM 22, M 20,
  S 16, L 5, N 17.

56. Family problems like divorce, parent-child conflict, etc.:
  VM 22, M 20, S 16, L 5, N 17.

57. What is the most important source of SWB for you personally (even if you do not now have it)? Your own self 34,
  other people 14, the Bible 1, God 7, Jesus Christ 7,
  other supernatural beings 0, nature 1, other (what?)
  (combinations mentioning God and/or Christ=10; others=
  4; NR=4.

For each of the following indicate whether you strongly agree,
agree, etc., that each of the items is necesary in order to have SWB:

58. To believe in life after death: SA 14, A 20, TA 21, TD 10,
  D 7, SD 10.

To believe in a Supreme Being: SA 27, A 20, TA 21, TD 1,
  D 6, SD 7.

To believe in Jesus Christ as one's own savior: SA 21, A 19,
  TA 17, TD 6, D 8, SD 11.

To believe in the goodness of all people: SA 13, A 30,
  TA 23, TD 3, D 7, SD 5.

To believe in the sinfulness of all people: SA 6, A 13,
  TA 16, TD 15, D 9, SD 23.

To believe in (what?) Oneself = 1; Jesus = 1; life after death = 1;
spiritual life = 1; humanity = 1; other responses = 11.

Evaluators of Spiritual Well-Being

59. Who are the best qualified persons to determine what spiritual well-being really is? Check each one that applies:

    <u>52</u> Ministers, priests, and rabbis

    <u>29</u> Psychiatrists and psychologists.

    <u>9</u> Medical doctors

    <u>6</u> Politicians and government officials

    <u>15</u> College professors

    <u>7</u> School teachers

    <u>38</u> Ordinary common people

    <u>62</u> Everyone is his or her own judge

    <u>6</u> Lawyers

    <u>7</u> Other

60. Now, go back over the above list and put a second check in front of the one, two, or three that are the *most important* persons to tell others what SWB is.

    (Ministers, priests, and rabbis = <u>28</u>; Everyone is his own judge = <u>27</u>; Ordinary common people = <u>15</u>; Psychiatrists and psychologists = <u>10</u>; College professors = <u>5</u>; Others = <u>10</u>; No response = <u>37</u>)

Background Information

61. How often do you attend religious services in a church or synagogue? At least once a week <u>31</u>; Once or more a month <u>22</u>; Several times a year <u>18</u>; Once a year or less <u>8</u>; Never <u>3</u>.

62. How often do you attend or take part in other religious activities, such as Bible studies, religious discussions, prayer groups, etc.? At least once a week <u>10</u>; Once or more a month <u>6</u>; Several times a year <u>12</u>; Once a year or less <u>21</u>; Never <u>31</u>. (No response = <u>2</u>)

63.   Are you a member of a church or synagogue? Yes _68_;
       No _12_. (NR = _2_)

64.   If no, have you ever been a church or synagogue member?
       Yes _13_; No _4_.

65.   What is your present or most recent denomination?
       Catholic _52_; Lutheran _10_; Other Protestant (which?) Presby-
       terian = _6_; Other Protestant = _8_; Eastern Orthodox _0_; Jew-
       ish _1_; Other _4_. (NR = _1_)

66.   Is your present church membership identity the same as that
       of your parents? Yes _68_; No _11_.

67.   In relationship to your parents, would you say that you are:
       More religious _16_; Less religious _35_; About the same _28_.
       (NR = _2_)

68.   How much education have you completed? Eight years or
       less _3_; 9 to 11 grades _0_; 12 grades (high school) _3_;
       1 to 3 years of college _36_; 4 years of college _33_; One or more
       years of graduate or professional studies beyond college _7_.

69.   What is your age? Under 18 _1_; 18-24 _70_; 25-39 _4_; 40-49 _2_;
       50-64 _2_; 65+ _3_.

70.   Are you: Male _39_, or Female _42_? (NR = _1_)

REFERENCES

Campbell, A., Converse, P.E., & Rodgers, W.L. *The quality of American life:
    Perceptions, evaluations, and satisfactions.* New York: Russell Sage Foun-
    dation, 1976.
Carrel, A. *Man, the unknown.* New York: Harper & Brothers, 1939.
Edwards, T.H., Jr., Mead, L.B., Palmer, P.J., & Simmons, J.P. *Spiritual growth:
    An empirical exploration of its meaning, sources, and implications.* Wash-
    ington, D.C.: Metropolitan Ecumenical Training Center, 1974.
Gerson, E.M. On "Quality of Life." *American Sociological Review,* 1976, *41*,
    793-806.
Glock, C.Y. On the study of religious commitment. *Religious Education,* 1962,
    57, S-98—S-110.
Krendel, E.S. Social indicators and urban systems dynamics. *Socio-Economic
    Planning Sciences,* 1971, *5*, 387-393.

Moberg, D.O. *Religion and personal adjustment in old age.* Unpublished doctoral dissertation, University of Minnesota, 1951. *Dissertation Abstracts,* 1952, 12, 341-342.

Moberg, D.O. Religiosity in old age. *The Gerontologist,* 1965, 5, 78-87.

Moberg, D.O. The encounter of scientific and religious values pertinent to man's spiritual nature. *Sociological Analysis,* 1967, 28, 22-33. (a)

Moberg, D.O. Science and spiritual nature of man. *Journal of the American Scientific Affiliation,* 1967, 19, 12-17. (b)

Moberg, D.O. Some findings and insights from my research on religion and aging. In J.E. Cantelon *et al.* (Eds), *Religion and aging: The behavioral and social sciences look at religion and aging.* Los Angeles: Rossmoor-Cortese Institute for the Study of Retirement and Aging, University of Southern California, 1967. Pp. 27-45. (c)

Moberg, D.O. *Spiritual well-being: Background and issues.* Washington, D.C.: White House Conference on Aging, 1971.

Moberg, D.O. Spiritual well-being in late life. In J.F. Gubrium (Ed.), *Late Life: Communities and environmental policy.* Springfield: Charles C Thomas, 1974. Pp. 256-279.

Moberg, D.O. Spiritual well-being: A challenge for interdisciplinary research. Paper presented at the annual meeting of the American Scientific Affiliation, San Diego, August 18, 1975.

Moberg, D.O., & Brusek, P.M. Spiritual well-being: A neglected subject in quality of life research. Paper presented at the annual meeting of the Midwest Sociological Society, Minneapolis, April 14, 1977.

NICA. *Spiritual well-being—a definition.* Athens, Ga.: National Interfaith Coalition on Aging, 1975.

Smith, D.M. *The geography of social well-being in the United States.* New York: McGraw-Hill, 1973.

U.S. Department of Health, Education, and Welfare. Toward a social report. Washington, D.C.: U.S. Government Printing Office, January 1969.

Chapter 5

SPIRITUAL WELL-BEING: A RELATIONSHIP THAT NURTURES

ROBERT I. KAHN

We have been exploring a definition of spiritual well-being, a definition especially for the elderly: "Spiritual well-being is the affirmation of life in a relationship with God, self, community and environment that nurtures and celebrates wholeness." The objective of this chapter is to examine the phrase "that nurtures and celebrates wholeness."

In biblical days, age was held in very high esteem. The aged were deemed worthy of honor by virtue of their longevity. After all, their longevity demonstrated their virtue. "Reverence for God prolongs man's days," says the book of Proverbs, and the book of Kings echoes: "If you walk in My ways, you will lengthen your days." A long life was the reward of a good life; therefore long life was proof of a good life.

To live long was to be blessed. The biblical writers regarded the days of old, before the Flood, as a kind of Golden Age in which human beings lived to an unbelievably ripe old age. In the early years of mankind's history, their history told them, it was not unusual for people to live more than nine centuries. Adam lived 930 years; Seth, 912; Jared, 962; and Methusaleh outlived them all, 969 years. The Golden Age, however, was not only in the past; it was to be in the future. In the ideal society, wrote Isaiah, the youngest will die at the age of one hundred. What a beautiful picture Zechariah paints with words as he prophesies that one day there will be old men and women sitting in the parks of Jerusalem while children play among them. In the Bible, age was deserving of honor.

This was not universally true in those ancient days nor everywhere in the world since. In Greece, with its accent on youth, old age was feared and even sometimes despised. On the

Greek island of Keos, for example, it is recorded that people would celebrate their sixtieth birthday with hemlock on the rocks. In pre-Christian Germany, the aged Teuton might request of his children that they slay him as an act of kindness. In savage tribes on Tahiti and Fiji, it is reported, retirement often took the form of suicide.

In the biblical world, however, old age was the crown of life. Ben Sira puts it so charmingly: "Like the lamp that shines upon the holy candlestick, so is the beauty of face in ripe age." The aged apparently presented no problem to biblical society. The responsibility for their care, if they needed it, devolved upon their families. To honor your father and mother included the obligation to provide their necessities. In a society in which the social unit was the patriarchal family, the aged had security until they died. There was no need for pension plans or old age assistance. The Bible nowhere states this, but there is a powerful argument from silence. The Bible is not silent about the needs of people; the Bible calls upon the social conscience of humanity. It summons people to care for the helpless; it specifies the widow, the orphan, the stranger, the prisoner in the dungeon, the poor, but it never once speaks of help for the aged. By its very silence, the Bible implies that growing old brought no insecurity.

The aged of biblical days did not require much social concern as to how they were to employ their time and energies. The only mention of retirement in the Bible refers to the Levites, who were to give up their sacred duties at the age of fifty-five, but whose financial status was secured by the Levitical tithes. In what was largely an agricultural and handcraft society, there was work for every member of the family, for the oldest as well as the youngest. Every member of the family had his part to perform, his share to contribute, and the dignity of knowing he was not useless.

Of course, they recognized that there was a diminishing contribution the aged could make. There is a discussion, in the book of Leviticus, as to how much a man shall pay when he vows his own value to God. In those days, as those who study the Bible will remember, men pledged to God a variety of gifts: livestock, children (remember Hannah and Samuel), and themselves. If a man vows himself to God, what is his obligation in monetary terms? For a man in the prime of life, the obligation was fifty shekels. At age sixty, however, the valuation dropped to fifteen. The important point is that it never dropped to zero; a human being had value, no matter what the number of years reached. "As strength is the beauty of youth, so grey hair is the crown of beauty to the aged." The aged must have been honored to be numbered among the elders who sat at the gate to be called upon by the virtue of their age, their dignity, and their experience to act as witnesses to agreements, juries in lawsuits, and advisers on matters of public concern.

In our day, however, old age is not so much a blessing as a problem. At one time we would have been the elders: now we are the elderly. There is so much of the Greek spirit in our time, of the accent on youth. Growing old, looking old, being old is regarded by many, old and young, as a burden, a curse, a vexation of spirit.

A biblical approach to old age in our time would begin with an attitude of reverence and gratitude for the gift of old age, not only by the old but by the young as well. A biblical approach would emphasize the dignity of the aged as individuals. If there is any truth the Bible emphasized again and again, it is that people must not be lumped together in groups, must not be separated into classes or castes, but must be treated as sacred personalities, as individuals, each created in the image of God.

This attitude should influence our retirement practices, our provisions for the healthy and capable elderly. It should also generate a compassion and concern for those elderly who are no longer able to care for themselves. The Bible was concerned for people, especially for those who had no one to care for them, to fend for them, to protect them. Today in that spirit, the biblical attitude would encompass the aged whose families cannot carry the full burden of their care. The elderly, well or ill, need the self-respect that derives from being usefully occupied, if possible, and warmly cared for. They need relationships with God, with self, and with community, which nurtures them in their old age.

It is in this biblical spirit that we now turn to the specific words in the definition of spiritual well-being: Nurture, celebration and wholeness. In introducing Hebrew words to illuminate nurture, celebration, and wholeness, we must explore not only the words but their roots.

Nurture, in English, is translated by the root of the Hebrew word, *Amen*. *Amen* is prominent in the vocabulary of religion. Its noun is *emunah*, which means faith. Its verb is *maamin*, which means to affirm. Its participle is *emet*, which means truth. Its use at the end of a prayer is like the seal of faith. However, the root of *amen* is *omen* and was used by Moses in one of his troubled dialogues with God in the book of Numbers. "Have I conceived this people?" he complained to God, "or given them birth that you should say to me, 'Carry them in thy bosom as an *omen*, a nursing father, carries a sucking child?'" The root of *amen* is nursing father, and how beautifully it illuminates the meaning of faith. Faith is the trust of an infant in its parents, it is the security felt by a child with his parents' arms about him. And, how rich it makes the biblical sentence: "Underneath are the everlasting arms."

Nurture, too, is rooted in the vocabulary of nursing, but the Hebrew root gives to the word nurture its religious dimension. It is God who nurtures us, who has endowed us with the powers of growth. In His nurture, we grow, we can grow, we ought to grow, all our lives.

Some would apply the law of entropy to human beings, saying that the day we are born we begin to die. This is nonsense. Man is not born to die, he is born to live, to grow. Death is not the goal of life, it is simply the end of it. Living is growing. Living defies the law of entropy. It may be true, in the world of physics, that there is a tendency in nature for heat or energy to be transferred until there is no more exchange, until nature reaches theoretical zero. However, life's processes run in precisely the opposite direction. Life organizes energy. From a single seed comes a marvelous growth. In human life, it is even more so, for not only do we grow in physical stature but in spiritual. Our intelligence, our imagination, our creativity continue to grow far beyond our physical maturity. Even if our bodies experience some negative entropy toward the end of life, the spirit can continue to our dying breath and beyond. William James, the pragmatist, who rejected the thought of immortality because he felt it had no useful function, began to reconsider it on his sixtieth birthday.

When someone asked him why his mind was ready for a change, his response was: "I am just becoming fit to live." Our faith in life can mature us; our *amens* can help us grow spiritually through a whole lifetime.

Here, again, the Bible has a word for us. Frequently the Bible pictures life as a passing moment, a dream, a tale that is told, a flower that fades, a cloud driven away by the wind. But in the book of Job, there is a figure of speech which far better describes the nurtured life, the life of growth. "You shall come to your grave in ripe age as a shock of corn comes in its season." How beautifully the author of Job says it: Old age is not withering, old age is ripening. It was in this same spirit that Robert Browning put into his poem *Rabbi Ben Ezra* that most beautiful vision of old age: "Grow old along with me! The best is yet to be, the last of life, for which the first was made: Our times are in His hand Who saith 'A whole I planned, Youth shows but half; trust God: see all nor be afraid!' "

How fruitful old age can be! All one has to do to recognize this is to review the work of Michelangelo, simply to compare the Pieta of his youth with the Pieta of his old age. The white marble masterpiece in the Vatican is world-famous. It is a magnificent work of art by a magnificent young artist. In terms of conception, technique, and achievement, it stands among the great art works of history. In the Cathedral in Florence though, down the side aisles past one altar after another, far to the back, there is a Pieta finished by Michelangelo when he was in his eighties. One cannot describe in words the impact of that group of figures. Michelangelo sculpted himself into that scene; he stands in back, a cowl over his head, looking on, and you see what he saw. After a lifetime of experience, having seen women weep over their dead sons, having seen death in many forms, having sensed the faith that that particular death could rouse in human beings, he speaks to the heart of pathos and compassion in ways that in his youth he could not. Grow old along with me, his career seems to say, the best is yet to be.

There is a community of the aged in Israel in the town of Pardes Hanah outside Tel Aviv. It is part a home for the aged, part a nursing home, but it is also a community. In this community, everyone who can be usefully employed is busy—not with busywork—but with real work. In the sewing room, abled-bodied elders, men and women, work at machines and by hand make sheets and pillowcases, the simple housedresses, nightgowns, and pajamas that they and their fellow residents wear. In the kitchen, residents of the home work at the tasks of cooking, baking, peeling, shelling, washing, drying, stacking, serving. This all comes into focus in the cobbler's shop, where an old man of 92 was busy putting half soles on a pair of worn shoes, and beside him was a younger man, only 72, whom the elder referred to as "my apprentice."

To live is to grow, to grow old is to ripen like a shock of corn in its season. Abraham was already 75 years old when he heard the call of God and struck out into new lands and new realms of the spirit to found the ethical monotheism that has been the spiritual seedbed of the Western world.

How are we to promote growth? How shall we nurture ourselves and each other, so that the best is yet to be? First of all, we need to take seriously the biblical principle of individualism and avoid any lockstep kind of thinking. Automatic and compulsory retirement, for example, is totally insensitive, wasteful of human resources, and destructive of human potential. Granted that sometimes people outlive their usefulness in certain jobs, but not all, and certainly not all at the same time. We are not and must not be prisoners of the calendar. Some men are productive into their eighties, others are old at sixty, but to put everyone on the Procrustes bed of sixty-five and out you go is to violate the spirit of our faith and of our democracy. For those who believe that old age is a time of ripening, of continued nurture and growth, the key word ought to be options, options that provide for all sorts of activity, whether useful or recreational, intellectual or physical, self-improving or society-improving.

There are so many potential options. Retired teachers can find classes anywhere they look. Retired craftsmen can train youngsters in a marketable skill. Retired businessmen can work with SCORE, helping young businessmen understand the fundamentals of marketing, stock control, bookkeeping, and profit-making.

In Houston, the Houston Metropolitan Ministries gives an opportunity for the aged to serve in the hospital as Foster Grandparents. They sit by bedsides in the childrens' wards; they sit in rocking chairs by babies' cribs and fondle, rock, pat and kiss their little charges. Useful? All of us know today that if a child does not receive the tender loving care expressed in fondling and holding, there is both a physical and emotional deprivation that results in more illness than the average, less development than the average, and more alienation than the average. Without expressed affection, a baby's growth is stunted. What a wonderful opportunity for these elders who may not have, or not have close at hand, grandchildren of their own. Fondling a baby not only gives nurture to the child; it nurtures the elderly as well. The story of the book of Ruth is an example. At the close of the story, Ruth the Moabite chose to follow her mother-in-law Naomi back to the land of Judea with the vow, "Your people shall be my people, and your God, my God." There, Ruth gleaned in the fields of Boaz and became his wife. Then she bore a child, a child who was to be the ancestor of David and through David, ancestor of the Messiah. The story continues, "And Naomi took the child and laid it in her bosom and became nurse to it." Her neighbors gathered round and fussed over the child in his grandmother's arms and exclaimed, "He shall be to you a restorer of life, and a nourisher of your old age." Who is nurturing whom? Nurture is growth, nurture is ripening like a shock of corn in its season. Nurture is saying Amen to life.

In Houston, there is a proposal to use public school facilities for programming for the elderly: the lunchrooms, the classrooms, and the school busses. The busses can be used to pick up the elderly and bring them to school cafeterias for a hot lunch, followed by group activities. Then they will have classroom options for continuing education, whether in skills, arts, crafts, or in general knowledge, and will take regular field trips to places of interest. Some will teach, some will learn, all will grow by sharing the ripening years.

There is no reason why this sort of program could not be established in almost every church. With imagination, with innovative programming, with the employment of available skills, there is no reason why we who have ripened like a shock of corn cannot be to each other masters and apprentices, a community of shared nurture. Ours must be the effort for ourselves and for others, of developing the structures that offer many options for people to continue to grow as long as they live.

Spiritual well-being is an affirmation of life in relationships that nurture and *celebrate*. The Hebrew word for celebration is the word *Chag*. That word describes the festivals; *Chag HaPesaach* is the Festival of Passover. Festival is not a good translation, it is too closely related to the word feast. *Chag* is more closely related to the Arabic *Hajj*, which means pilgrimage, and of course the pilgrimage is a feature of the Jewish festivals when all the population of ancient Israel would come up to Jerusalem, bring their lambs on the *Chag* called passover, their first fruits on the *Chag* called Pentecost, and their harvest on the *Chag* called Booths.

The root of the Hebrew word *Chag* means circle. A derivative, *Chug*, is used in modern Hebrew to designate a study circle. In its origins, it seems to have referred to a kind of circling sacred dance. What a beautiful picture this conjures up: the meaningful round of the year from seedtime to harvest, from the night of winter to the light of spring, and the sacred round of life in the pilgrimage from birth to death, in which we by celebration "crown moments of life with meaning."

After all, we live by symbols, by ceremonies, by celebrations. Everything we truly cherish, every value we hold high, every significant event in the year and in the years of a lifetime, is symbolized and celebrated through those symbols. In every civilization and in every religion, human hearts and minds have developed and devised rites of passage for the lifetime of a human being, celebrations that symbolize the stages of life and the values of life. As adolescence begins, the Indian lad would undertake a kind of wilderness survival test along with a hill-top meditation; a Jewish boy would come up to the altar to read from the scrolls of the Torah; a Christian would be confirmed. Growing up is a serious business and must be celebrated, otherwise how is a youngster to know what it means to become an adult?

We need to develop some kind of a rite of passage to the harvest years of life, the years when we ripen like a shock of corn in its season. We have something of the sort. We observe sixtieth, sixty-fifth, and seventieth birthdays with more than the usual celebration. If we have been long in the employ of a company or corporation, they may give us a banquet and present us with a gold watch. However, we need to invent a *chag*, a sacred ceremony, that will speak to the heart about the meaning of time as it passes, about the meaning of the evening of life.

Perhaps our society needs a philosophy, too, in the existential sense. Usually we think of philosophy as a sort of leisurely discussion of life's meaning while we sit on a porch rocking and smoking a pipe, and looking out across the hills, in consideration of life and its import. An existential philosophy, though, is in a far different mood. It is as though a person were to come out of the doctor's office with the doctor's words ringing in his ears, "There is nothing that can be done for you. You have a year, maybe two years, to live." That person begins to think about the meaning of life in an entirely different way.

Somehow, a celebration of the achievement of age ought to include such existential thinking, ought to include the kind of symbolism, the kind of poetry, the kind of sacred round, which would inspire thought about the years ahead, about how to live those remaining years in spiritual well-being.

There is another Hebrew word for celebrate. It is *Hallel*. It can be recognized as part of the Psalmist's term: *Hallelujah*. Its root means to shine; in the intensive form of *Hallel*, it means to flash a light, to illuminate, to hold up to view, to celebrate. What is it that we seek to illuminate, to hold up to view, to celebrate? The wholeness of life.

It is this wholeness, the last word in our definition of spiritual well-being, that ties it all together, that weaves together all of the relationships, to God, to self, to community, to environment. It was such wholeness that Carlyle celebrated when he spoke of invisible filaments that tie all things together so that if you tug at any one point you create a tremor through the whole. This sense of wholeness must permeate our thinking, both in considering ends and means, so that we do not pigeonhole our problems, segregate issues, or reduce our efforts to mere tinkering with parts.

This wholeness is the emphasis of our time, or should be. In a world in which specialization has fragmented almost every part of life, we need the sense of the whole to guide us. This is what ecology is about: the interrelatedness of all nature. This is the reason for renewed emphasis upon the family doctor, the effort to see man as a whole. This is the new emphasis in psychiatry, that people do not live in isolation. A human being with a problem has that problem in his relationships to others and the whole family needs to be treated.

Wholeness. Again the Hebrew language comes to our aid. In Hebrew, wholeness is rendered by the word *Shalom. Shalom* means complete. *Shalom* also means peace, which provides an important contrast in meanings. Peace comes from the Latin word *Pax*, which also gives us Pact. Peace is a kind of pact, a relationship between wars so to speak. *Shalom*, on the other hand, is completeness, wholeness, the truest form of peace. *Shalom* also means well-being. When you ask someone, *Mah Shlomcha*, it is rather like saying, "how do you do," but its true meaning is "How is your well-being?" So, we have bracketed our definition. Spiritual well-being, spiritual *shalom*, is an affirmation of faith that celebrates life.

Let us illustrate the wholeness implied by *shalom* by one of its uses in a different context. In speaking of Jewish family life, we often use the term *Shalom Bait*, the well-being of the home, a peaceful home, as it were. To many men, a peaceful home is one in which the wife never asks for money and the children are quiet, but *shalom bait* is a different kind of peace, a peace that comes from balance, from unity, from what might be called a family-centered household. All of us are acquainted with the patriarchal family in which the father was master, whose favor was curried and whose word was obeyed. There was the matriarchal family in which the source of authority was the mother. In modern times, we have seen the child-centered family in which the parents quail before the will of the children. *Shalom bait* describes a family-centered family, a family in which husband and wife are agreed on the values of life, in which the hearts of children are turned to parents and the hearts of parents to children, in which the youngsters share with each other. *Shalom bait* describes a family that celebrates together, birthdays and anniversaries, holidays and holy days. *Shalom bait* describes a family in which each member is concerned for all others, and all are concerned for the one who needs it most.

If one simply extends the concept of *shalom bait* to include the human family, and the world-home in which we all live, then the same principles of wholeness become very precious, and our relationships reach out to the very edge of the universe. Think of a world-centered world of people in which all of our relationships, to God, to self, to community, and to environment are balanced off against each other, in which we nurture and celebrate wholeness.

Our relationship to God is central. We are called upon to love the Lord our God with all our hearts, with all our soul, with all our might, but the love of God can be out of balance if it is our only love. Our love of self does not usually need any encouragement; if anything, our absorption in ourselves requires discouraging. However, there is the temptation to self-denial, to a sort of martyr's role in which a mother works herself to death for her children, a businessman works himself to death for his family's security, a minister neglects his health and his family's emotional needs in service to others. Respect for self, for our bodies' needs, our minds' renewal, our hearts' hunger, our souls' health is part of the *shalom* we seek.

So, too, with the community and our relationship to it. There is a pattern of thought that puts the community in second place to self, a far second place. Survival is the first law of nature. "Winning is everything!" We need the advice of Hillel from long ago: "If I am not for myself, who will be for me, but if I am for myself alone, what am I?" However, this whole world is our home; this universe, and every part of it. We are formed by the same forces, chemical, physical, and spiritual, that hold the stars in their orbit, thrust up the mountains, scoop out the seas, bring the rose to bloom, teach the hawk to fly and the horse to neigh. "If I climb up into heaven, behold Thou art there, and If I go to the ends of the earth, behold Thou art there." The *shalom*, the wholeness of this world-home depends upon our balancing all our relationships in creative tension and nurturing them in wholeness.

These older years are precious years, precious for us and precious for our juniors. Browning celebrated old age, the vintage years, the ripening years, the years when experience and wisdom all add to the beauty and spiritual well-being of life. The older we grow, the more serene we should become, the more we should recognize the experiences of life as a refining and deepening process, so that we become radiating centers of life's wisdom and help younger people face the future with faith.

We live in time, but time is the part of which the timeless is the whole, so that even as life comes to an end in time it continues in eternity. We can see beyond the grave and outlive our mortality. Leo Baeck, heroic German rabbi, who chose to remain with his people in the gathering storm rather than accept proffered pulpits in the free world, said, at the Bar Mitzvah of his grandson, that human beings are the only creatures we know who recognize their grandchildren. It is this that motivates our talk of leaving the world a better place for posterity. We live in time, we think in terms of the timeless.

We live in time and in eternity. The wholeness of life is not a static totality, but a growing universe of value that extends far beyond our brief years. Beyond the grave there is life everlasting, for we human beings are overendowed for a purely temporal and biological life. All of the other creatures of the world are equipped with only those qualitites necessary to physical survival both of self and of species. There is no waste structure in a tree, no unused parts in a chicken or a rabbit. Everything is given to insure biological survival and no more. Humanity has qualities not really necessary to human survival. We may need shelter from the elements to survive, but Greek columns, Gothic arches, and the designs of Frank Lloyd Wright are not necessary merely to survive. These satisfy non-biological hungers of the human heart. We do not need love to reproduce our young—sex will do it—yet long beyond the years of reproduction affectionate love lights up our days and nurtures our hearts. In these aspects of life, and in so many others, we participate in the timeless qualities of beauty, goodness, and truth. Whatever life beyond the grave may be like (of this we can only speculate) this we know: we begin our immortality where we leave off our mortality. Our task, therefore, should be not only to leave the world a better place but also to leave the world a better person.

This wholeness is organic: we do not impose it upon nature as the product of our pattern-producing minds; on the contrary, the patterned thought of our brains reflects the patterns of nature itself. Wholeness is a spiritual rather than intellectual quality that binds together the we and "non-we," the human and non-human, the present and the eternal, the creation and the Creator. Deep within us is a vision of wholeness, of what the world might be, could be, should be. We are, each of us, parts of the whole, the wholeness of the human community—all brothers under God— the wholeness of the physical world—the environment in which we dwell, the wholeness of the Creator who flung out the stars across the light years and yet leans down close to the suffering to hear their cry, the wholeness in which we live, by which we are nurtured, and whose wonder and beauty we celebrate.

Our Spiritual Well-Being is an affirmation of life in relationship with God, with self, with community and with environment, which nurtures and celebrates wholeness. In affirming that faith in the One, we affirm our faith in each one. In the wholeness of His unity, no one is alone and every life finds purpose.

Chapter 6

SPIRITUAL WELL-BEING OF THE ELDERLY: A RATIONALE FOR SEMINARY EDUCATION

PAUL B. MAVES

Our task in this section is to discuss six questions related to the church and spiritual well-being of the aged. First we should ask: Why should the churches be interested in the field of aging, especially? Second, we will discuss: How should the church be related to the field of gerontology, or related to work with the aging? The third area deals with why the church has been so slow to pick up on this field, which is now almost half a century old. Then, fourth, we will discuss why the clergy need to be specially equipped for a ministry with the aging when they graduate from theological school. The fifth question has to do with what skills and attitudes are needed by the clergy or people who work with older people, from the standpoint of fostering spiritual well-being? Finally, we will indicate, very briefly, what areas of knowledge students should be exposed to in the seminary curriculum. Our objective, then, is to discover some ways whereby the seminary can help clergy to become equipped with the necessary knowledge and attitudes and skills for ministry with the aging.

Educators in our seminaries and schools of theology may have some skepticism, and rightly so, about the proposal that one more course be introduced for a new field of specialization, or academic discipline, into the theological seminary. The history of American theological education is a story of a struggle to introduce into the curriculum emerging fields of knowledge and emerging technologies of helping. A primary concern has been the integration of the theological curriculum, because of the real problem of getting all the important things into the three years of coursework. The questioning and the resistance, while it is very irritating to the innovator, is an important part of the sorting out process, and that is really important. When Henry Wadsworth Longfellow was brought onto the faculty of Harvard, he encountered all kinds of rejection and resistance because his job was to introduce the teaching of modern languages, like French and German, into the curriculum. It was an unheard of innovation. The other professions are facing the same kind of pressures. Medical colleges are under pressure to introduce courses in geriatrics so that doctors will know more about the diseases of the elderly. The same thing is true of nurses and lawyers, and other professions.

Why should religious bodies, then, take special notice of the phenomenon of aging and the situation of the aged in our society? The first and most obvious answer to that question is that we are living and have lived through a silent revolution, which can be ignored only at the point of being completely irrelevant. Since 1900, a quarter century has been added to the average life. This means that people now live on past the age of childbearing and childrearing; it means that they live on past the age of productive, remunerative employment. What is the meaning of Christian vocation for all these additional years that have been added to the average human life? The percentage of older persons in the population has gone from 4 percent in 1900 to 10.5 today, and probably to 12.5 percent in the year 2000. What does this mean in terms of political power? The protests of the 60s and 70s by the youth may be nothing to what will be seen within a decade in this country from the older people who have become conscious of the fact that they have been short-changed of some of the goods of society to which they might feel they are entitled. Along with this, of course, because of our shift from an agrarian society to an industrial society, we have instituted the policy of mandatory retirement. This is a new thing in human history. The tapering off process, which was common on the farm, has been replaced by the cutting off process. This means a cut in income, about 50 percent on the average, a loss of freedom that goes along with a cut in income, the freedom to travel, to contribute, to buy things. It means a loss of status. It means the loss of opportunity for social interaction and, finally, the loss of a significant social role. It means a waste of human resources.

Religious bodies ought to be concerned with aging, with the situation of the elderly, because the question that Robert Butler raised in the title of his book *Why Survive?* (1975) is a theological question that can only be answered by faith. It cannot be answered by scientific studies—it is a value judgment. As a religious vision of life, we are called upon to incarnate or embody that vision, and as custodians of a message about the ultimate value of all life and its eternal significance, we will want to communicate it. This challenges the church to be concerned about the interpretation of the meaning of life.

Sociologically, churches provide religious functions in society. Most organizations provide primary functions and secondary functions. The primary functions are those for which they basically exist or came into being and the secondary functions are those they tend to accrue, or that develop as a concomitant to their existence. Occasionally, the second functions come to predominate if the original purpose is forgotten or is no longer valid. The tendency of congregations to become social clubs, for example, providing opportunities for friendship and fellowship and so forth, is an illustration of this. Theologically speaking, the church was called into being by God for a particular purpose. The clarification of this purpose and its implications for a particular group in a particular situation is the first step in our ministry. The church's primary function is to promulgate values and a vision of life. Its primary function is to provide an interpretation of events that can make life meaningful in the face of its fundamental absurdities.

In its ministry with aging the church too often concentrates upon the secondary function of a religious group, being content to provide social services to the elderly such as senior citizens' clubs, noon-day meals, meals on wheels, and other useful and often essential and deeply appreciated services. Unfortunately, the church often does this while failing to establish its theological rationale for such services and failing to challenge the prevailing social norms or values that might lead to providing such services quite differently, or might even make them unnecessary. For example, if all people had a decent system of income maintenance we would not have to have discounts, we would not have to have demeaning golden-age cards, and people would not have to be stopped at the admission desk and told "Oh you can get in cheaper than that because you're now over 65."

For Christians, the church is intended to be the body of the Christ through which the Spirit finds effective expression in the present. The living church is encountered as one meets and participates in the fellowship of disciples who try to follow the way. It is through their relationship with and within that body that persons are sustained and transformed. It has been written that we are formed, we are deformed, and we are transformed by our relationships. The new birth takes place when we enter into the new set of relationships, very particular kinds of relationships. That is when we are regenerated—we expose ourselves to the possibility of being converted. The church is moved by the Spirit that empowers it to preach good news to the poor, to free the captives, to give sight to the blind, to let the broken victims go free, and to proclaim the year of the Lord's favor. The elderly are recipients of God's love. They too are called to His service, so the church includes the elderly. It seeks to meet their needs, it enlists their talents in their mission.

Why has the church been so slow to respond? As long as it was preoccupied with institutional maintenance and growth, the church has tended to seek out and curry favor with the young, the prosperous, and the powerful in order to enhance its own status. The exception, of course, has been the wealthy who are donors to worthy causes. Pastors and church leaders are trained in and committed to the programs and approaches that have been institutionalized by denominations—their boards and agencies and techniques and literature and audiovisual aids and all the things that institutionalize certain kinds of ministries. Pastors have found it hard to take on additional responsibilities, they are already overworked; they have been taught to function in particular ways and to do particular things. Also, churches were often captive to a fragmented view of man and a bifurcated view of the world. Too often the church was interested only in the soul or the life to come. Further, all of us have been immersed in and captivated by a cultural value system that unconsciously demeans the elderly, fears old age, and sees little point to saving spent lives.

Finally, the elderly, like the poor, tend to become invisible. If because of physical infirmity or lack of transportation they tend to drop out of attendance at church services, they are soon forgotten. If they move when they retire, they tend to find it very difficult to get reinvolved in the new church community.

Our task, then, is to see how the elderly are to be involved in and related to the church and what the role of the church to the elderly is to be. There are four essential processes that must go on within the congregation if it is a live organization true to its calling. The first process is creating the caring community, the *koinonia*. The caring community emerges when there is opportunity for frequent, warm, close personal interaction and sufficient time is spent together for the relationship to develop. Just being with other people long enough and often enough in a relaxed enough setting is necessary for a relationship to develop. Groups must be small enough for each member to participate in the process of communication. There must be time for give and take. There must be a feeling of acceptance, of being valued and of belonging. Another condition is that there is a tolerance for diversity and eccentricity as well as a capacity for constructive conflict. Just because people get older is no sign that they are easier to live with. In fact, they very frequently have less need to keep up pretenses and speak more openly and bluntly and honestly and sometimes more hurtfully.

The caring community probably demands what Alvin Toffler calls transition groups in his book *Future Shock* (1970), where persons who are in similar predicaments or going through similar changes can share with and support each other. Groups for widows, divorcees, recent retirees, and cancer victims are illustrations of the kinds of transition groups that may be useful. Experience in these may well make it possible for members to move into nurture groups. An eighty-two-year-old lady in a nursing home, who was once a YWCA secretary and high school teacher, wrote in a letter, "Four of us have formed a little club. We meet once a week to share our experiences so we can keep on growing." One way we devaluate the elderly is to think of them solely as subjects of our ministry, rather than as participants with us in ministry. Another way is to forget that those who do the work of the congregation are themselves in need of nurturing and support.

A second essential process that contributes to the vitality of the church is that of translating and celebrating the faith tradition in contemporary terms. This is the process of representing the biblical story as an illumination of our own history, using every artistic device at our disposal. It involves comprehending experience in significant patterns of meaning through reflection. It is the sharing of a message of hope, the *kerygma*, based upon a transcendent vision. It is the sanctioning and celebration of a way of life based upon that vision. Older people can participate in translating, expressing, and celebrating the faith tradition as leaders of worship, interpreters of God's word as it comes through the scripture and history and through their own history. They can participate in expressing the faith through art in music, poetry, painting, banners, and dance.

A third process is that of empowering and equipping the members of the congregation. This function focuses on personal growth and spiritual development. This is the teaching function. The Apostle Paul wrote to the Philippians: "It is my prayer that your love may abound more and more, with knowledge and all discernment so that you may approve what is excellent and may be pure and blameless for the day of Christ, filled with the fruits of righteousness which come through Jesus Christ, to the glory and praise of God" (Phil. 1:9-11).

A fourth process is that of changing the world through organizational and political action—community development and political action. It includes the search for the basis of a viable social order or a form of community that is congruent with the transcedent vision of the Kingdom of God. This demands that we wrestle with the question of maintenance of income during the years of retirement. We live in a world in which the disparity of wealth between those who have and those who have not has become increasingly glaring.

Having given some reasons why the church should be especially concerned with the ministry with the aging, we will now turn to the question of why clergy need to be especially trained to participate in and lead a ministry of congregations with the elderly. First of all, pastors need to be prepared to help persons cope with the crisis and stress that arise throughout the entire span of life. They need to be introduced to the knowledge that children leave home and people go through "empty-nest" stages, and there are changes of careers. They need to know something about the stresses of moving, divorce, bereavement, and widowhood and need to be helped to see the total span of life and some of its expectancies.

Pastors have been children, they have been youth, and they have been young adults, but when they graduate from seminary very few of them have experienced living through middle years and almost none of them the later years. Most of our seminaries would not accept students who are over sixty-five. Therefore, while they can draw on their own experience for some insight into the experiences of the younger parishioners, they cannot do so with older persons. They need some help to learn how to empathize with people who have gone through things they have not yet encountered.

Many pastors have assimilated the negative assumptions and stereotypes about the later years that distort their relationships with the elderly. Pastors need to be confronted with and freed as much as possible from inaccurate and destructive images and stereotypes. Maybe they ought to have the experience of putting on glasses that distort vision—like cataracts or loss of side vision.

To be more specific, one of the attitudes the pastor ought to be exposed to is acceptance of persons who have value not for what they have done, not because of what they may be able to contribute, not because of the status they had occupied, but because they are human beings, persons who have a future. Second is a recognition of the dignity to which they are entitled as human beings, as well as the respect they have earned by years of living. Third, there needs to be a willingness to bestow upon the elderly the gift of taking time to listen and of trying to hear without judging. Working with older people means bridging a cultural gap. Pastors who come out of seminary need some assistance in learning to live with other cultures and bridging these cultural gaps. This is the kind of thing missionaries have to learn when they go to a foreign culture. Fourth is the readiness to take responsibility for others openly, to the degree to which others consent, neither overprotecting nor leaving them unsupported. That is a difficult situation because there comes a time when decisions have to be made for other people; it is difficult to be able to do it in such a way that it is not demeaning. The fifth thing is being prepared to invite older people to participate, to get involved in making decisions and carrying out programs, particularly those that affect their own destiny.

One last thing. We have discussed the need to understand the cycle of human development, aging and dying, the social aspects of gerontology, the agencies to meet the needs of older persons, and ways of assessing the needs of a community. Finally, pastors need a theology that relates faith to loss, bereavement, struggle, suffering, failure, and dying that provides for the celebration of grace. It is a faith that can allow one to see the humor in life and to laugh at the absurd, a faith that allows one to be surprised at wonder without needing to have all the answers. Some of this is not taught—it is given. Some of it can only be learned by living with the mind opened to new insights. We need to pool our experience in the congregation of the people of God so that we can live faithfully and gracefully all the way through life.

REFERENCES

Butler, Robert N. *Why survive? Being old in America.* New York: Harper and Row, 1975.

Toffler, Alvin. *Future shock.* New York: Random House, 1970.

Section II
SPIRITUAL WELL-BEING IN RELATION TO GOD

Chapter 7

SPIRITUAL WELL-BEING OF THE ELDERLY IN RELATION TO GOD

CHARLES J. FAHEY

When it comes to the question of holiness, we know of no religious group or denomination that makes it age-related. A quest for holiness is a lifelong task and is as much of a challenge to the old as it is to the young.

In terms of a personal relationship to our Creator, it would seem that there are at least five elements that are involved in virtually all of our religious groups. Spirituality at its very essence involves a call to prayer. This is an act in which an individual will use his or her internal faculties to develop a consciousness of God's presence. Second, there is endemic to the very notion of spirituality a commitment to common prayer, that is, praying with others in formal or informal settings. A third area essential to the notion of holiness is the idea of moral behavior based upon religious traditions. Love the Lord our God with all mind and heart and soul; love our neighbor as ourself. Unfortunately, the culture of which we are a part tends to speak of love as being a provenance of the young, and yet this twofold law of love is equally as applicable to the seventy-year-old as it is to the seventeen-year-old.

The fourth area is the role of persons in regard to their neighbors, which we sum up in the word witness. Often it is a misstatement that the future of the church is in the hands of the young. Rather, we might say that it is in the hands of the old. If old people view life, with its limitations and with its heartaches, within a spiritual context and with enthusiasm, then they are giving a kind of witness to the validity of religious thought that no young person can ever give. On the other hand, if a person who is older and who has been identified with religion for many years seems to have a narrow perspective in regard to life, shows

61

an intolerance or self-centeredness, then religious views held by
that person tend to be rendered incredible in the eyes of the young.
The last concept in this overall framework of looking at holiness,
in addition to personal prayer, community prayer, moral behavior based upon revelation, and the witness obligation of those
who are believers, would be the question of the communication
of religion to the younger generation. In other cultures it has been
particularly the role of the old to pass on wisdom. Of course,
when it comes to religion, this becomes a responsibility of those
who have spent a lifetime of integrating religious truths into
their own lives, to communicate this in a formal, substantive way
to younger generations.

As long as there is something to be learned about the
intrapsychic function of man, or about the universe in which we
live, there remains the responsibility on the church, as a
community of faith, to integrate these new revelations with that
which is old. There are those among us who in the name of
integrity of revelation refuse to recognize the new revelation that
is in our midst, and yet it is to the peril of the church and to the
peril of revelation itself not to integrate or transmit it. A
particularly important part of the spirituality of the old is to
undertake this kind of reflective integration and transmission of
the faith as it is known.

One of the insights of our own day is to recognize that behavior
is influenced greatly by a number of social structures, whether it
be the family, society, or the culture. We recognize that these
things have a tremendous amount of influence on us. There are
those social structures that might be viewed as virtuous, and there
are social structures and cultural values that can only be termed
as sinful. There are times that the behavior of the church itself is
sinful, particularly in the way that the church itself receives older
persons. All too often the church succumbs to the culture of
which we are a part. The church itself segregates. The church
itself can keep older persons apart.

Ministries to older persons in the overall life of the church all
too often are neglected. Our ministry is to youth, or to this group,
or to that group, not recognizing that there should be a ministry
to the old and of the old, that older persons should be an integral

part of the church. Man was made in the image and likeness of God, and man is in that image and likeness when he is free. It is the responsibility of the Church to be aware of all those things that diminish human freedom, including sickness, ignorance, and psychological illness, or external oppressiveness, poverty, or political repression. It is the responsibility of the Church to help men to be free and self-determining, because to the degree to which they are free and self-determining they are acting in the image of God. This theology of liberation serves as a criterion against which we can measure our activity, whether it be a direct service activity, a social action activity, or an internal church activity.

Chapter 8

THEOLOGY FOR AGING
CARL G. HOWIE

I t would be pretentious to suggest that within this brief chapter it would be possible to fashion a total theology for aging. At the outset let it be clearly understood that there is no specific theology for aging that differs from a theology for youth or for marriage or for society. Theology is an exercise in seeing and understanding life in its totality or in any segment in the light of God. The purpose here is to discover how affirmations and assumptions of theological thought should in particular inform the experience for aging. The writer is convinced that a non-Christian, erroneous theology lies behind existing attitudes toward the aging in our society and is sometimes acted out both by other age groups and the aged themselves. There is, in fact, a a Christian heresy behind many contemporary, widespread attitudes among and toward the aging. This chapter, therefore, is not meant to be an academic exercise in doctrinaire theology, but a quest for redemption through recovery and acceptance of assumptions that are God-given.

A basic assumption in Christian theology is that *God is the Creator.* By his action life is shaped, and by his gift man becomes a living being. According to the most traditional doctrine, man was created in the image of God. To be sure, there has been almost continuous discussion of what constitutes this image and likeness. Some hold that self-conscious life is the image, while others insist that the divine part of human makeup is the individual's ability to think beyond himself, that is, to think abstractly. Self-transcendence itself may well be the divine spark that is the basic human quality. To dream, to hope, and to imagine are marks of humanity. Still others identify the image of God with our capacity and need for relationship. Human life must be a social experience to be true life. There have been countless other suggestions. However one may decide to identify the image of

God, that image is not a human attainment; it is a gift. Value has been placed on us by the Creator. As writers of the Declaration of Independence put it, all are "endowed by their Creator with certain unalienable rights." Value, therefore, is primarily identified with being, not with doing. That value neither diminishes with the onset of age nor with reduction of activity. In other words, it is not what one does, but who one is that gives value.

This worth that God has given to every man and woman was reinforced by the life and ministry of Jesus of Nazareth. Through the mystery of incarnation, God became a member of the human family. In light of this incarnation, no doubt about the lasting value and worth of human life could stand. Men and women are now seen as the sons and daughters of God. This is not an attainment, it is a gift, a heritage that cannot be set aside except by wrongheadedness. God has set his love upon persons, has accepted them as his own. In sum, value and worth are a divine endowment, not a human attainment.

Yet the society of which we are a part is primarily a society of doing, not of being. For example, the first question put by most people upon meeting a stranger is, "What do you do?" Almost without exception an individual is quickly identified and valued by what he or she does. With the young, most are likely to ask, "What are you going to be?" Actually the question is, "What activity is going to give you your identity?" A young senator who was showing some older people around the Houses of Congress turned and patronizingly asked one of the group, "And what did you used to be?" The older man curtly and insistently answered, "I still am." (Comfort, 1976)

This society frequently does not value people on the basis of their being as persons but according to their activity. As a result, when that activity diminishes, then personal value is also said to diminish. Frenetic activity is identified as the mark of true life; hence, when activity is either cut back or changed, the person to whom this happens is regarded as a non-person. In the words of Paul Tournier (1972): "A man asks me: 'Who are you?' I reply, 'I am a doctor.' 'Yes,' he says, 'I know, but who are you?' At the age of action, I am defined by my function, by what I do. As age comes, this function, this doing gradually ceases to define me. I have to define myself in terms of what I am." (p. 210-211)

There is, then, a Christian heresy built into contemporary life that holds that man is man or woman is woman only so long as he or she can produce children or make things. The final conclusion of such an assumption is that people become things that can be discarded when they no longer have full productive power.

The harsh truth is that the basic affirmation of Christian faith has been ignored in the devaluation of people who become inactive. If they have ever had life and value, they still have it because it is the gift of God. That value is not diminished with age. What is wrong is the system that tends to devalue all persons.

Jesus in his ministry came to give back value and self-esteem to people who had been devalued by society. God has made each person "somebody." Never should anyone be able to take away that gift of value that is the property of each person by creation. The truth is that an aging person is the same person he or she was in younger days. Identity has not changed; only the exterior is altered. There is no deterioration of being, only a change of body. The Apostle Paul gives an insight into this fact of experience in his word to the church at Corinth, "Though the outer man of ours may be falling into decay, the inner man is being renewed day by day" (II Corinthians 4:16).

Man's life is imperfect; human beings are flawed or incomplete. In general this condition, which has been theologically defined by the word "sin," is identified with rebellion. That rebellion takes the form, according to the Genesis account, of wanting to be more than human or not being satisfied with being merely human. It is a pretense that human life is not limited by time and space. The stories of the Fall in the Garden of Eden and the Tower of Babel describe this part of the human condition. This flawed human condition is not to be found exclusively in either the young or the old; it is the general human condition. In order to find completion, there must be intervention from beyond by God's coming into life and by good relationship to others. By this, emptiness is filled and incompleteness moves toward completion.

Redemption involves recognition of dependence on God and on others for life. It also requires coming to grips with mortality and other limits set on all of human life. As it relates to age, redemption allows persons to live with unfinished projects and unanswered questions. It is, then, possible to admit the reality of death and the incompleteness of life. There is a lessening of anxiety about time running out and greater joy in the precious- ness of remaining time.Redemption comes through Jesus Christ, who has made each a somebody. That is the basic affirmation of the gospel. Those whom others call "nobodies," non-persons, have become "new creations," somebodies, in Jesus Christ. God does not change this process with age, and so those who have faith can, in some measure, counter the societal tendency of making them non-persons. Despite restrictive life and diminished acti- vity, it is possible to know that our labor is not vain in the Lord. Redemption results in reduction of anxiety because of the firm belief that God can and does use any life in his service at any of its progressive stages.

Since life is a gift, living must be a stewardship. All of life is God's gift, not just its early years. Each phase of life has its burdens and opportunities, and later life is no exception. The question is how to fulfill the specific stewardship that devolves upon the aged, not how to deny that it happens. The first part of this stewardship is recognition that every day of life, not just the early or youthful days, is God's gift. All times are God's time. Unfortunately, many see and define the latter days as burden, not as adventure. As a result, they grow weary with the burden instead of rejoicing in the gift. Days are spent waiting in inactivity for life to end. Old minds atrophy from disuse. Aging hearts draw back from involvement, fearing that the strain may be too much, and are dwarfed. For those who accept each new day as a divine gift to be used, life is renewed.

Independence and problem solving can and often are the keys to continued self-esteem. So long as there are mental and physical capacities with which to do so, the aged should take care of their own affairs and maintain responsibility for themselves. In other words, they ought to be stewards of their own lives and refuse to give over that personal management to some other individual or group. Personal decisions and self-directed activities are basic to wholesome life.

Another crucial point in any theology for aging is the acceptance of aging, not as a curse but as a normal stage of development. To accept age as part of the divine gift of life makes the aged understand their state of being as a true call to specific stewardship. The truth is that, far from being helpless, the aged can and regularly do add a dimension to life that would otherwise be missing. They perform many functions that cannot be done by the young or by those overly active in middle years.

Older people become the living books from which all must learn. They reach back beyond the experience of the young to the times before, and thus enrich all lives by sharing their memories. With the longer perspective and the time for knowledge to become wisdom, they have a better insight into and vision of life than others may have. They know that the great moments in life were not in the earthquake or fire and wind of great events, but in quietness before God.

The aged have a responsibility to help free others from the belief that frenetic activity is the measure of life. Perhaps they can restore some measure of sanity to a society that is so busy doing that its people have lost value in being. By maintaining their integrity and value, the aged bear witness to the undiminished worth that God attaches to human life itself. It is part of the stewardship of the aging to teach younger persons not how to make things or how to run a technological world but, rather, through sharing, to try to give some insight into what is enduring and what is ephemeral in experience. The kind of wisdom to which reference is made here is reflected in the words of the late Supreme Court Justice Learned Hand, as cited by Lester Pearson (1970):

> You may build your Towers of Babel to the clouds, you may contrive ingenuously to circumvent nature by devices beyond even the understanding of all but a handful; you may provide endless distractions to escape the tedium of your barren lives; you may rummage the whole planet for your ease and comfort. It will avail you nothing; the more you struggle, the more deeply you will be enmeshed. Not until you have the courage to meet yourselves face to face, to take true account of what you find, to respect the sum of the account for itself and not for what it may bring you, deeply to believe that each of you is a holy vessel unique and

irreplaceable; only then will you have taken the first steps along the
pathway of wisdom. (p. 133)

To fulfill this responsibility and stewardship requires that the
old not ape the young. Too often these days older people·are told
that they must "keep young." To be sure, physical exercise and
intellectual interests are vital to keeping life human, but for the
aged to delude themselves about age is ridiculous. Age should be
worn as a mantle of glory. One should not hide it but rather be
proud of it. Until there is a pride in age by the aged, it will
continue to be treated as a punishment and as if it were some
terrible sickness.

The aged need not believe that life is defined only by motion.
There is no reason for an older person to engage in square
dancing, for instance, unless that is something he or she wants to
do. Whatever else the aged should do, they should never let
anyone demand some kind of youthful activity from them in
order to prove their worth and aliveness.

With the onset of age, the end of life, death, which is the final
devaluation, is inevitably drawing closer. However, according to
the Christian faith, there is hope of resurrection. This earthly
house will be dissolved. Materials used for a time will be
redistributed into the natural cycle. Still the promise is simple:
God will recreate each by resurrection from the emptiness of
death to new life.

Men and women in the later years of life move definitely toward
fulfillment of promise. Life will go through a transition called
death so that, like a grain of wheat, it may grow into a greater
harvest. That which persons have known only in measure they
shall know in greater measure in the next stage of the adventure.
Thus death has been called the final stage of growth and so it is.
Asquith (1970) maintains that death must be understood as a part
of the life experience and adventure. "Death, then, can be seen as
all right when it comes as a normal conclusion of life. It should
appear not as a surprise, as something fearful or dreadful, or as
something unwanted, but as something that has always been
plainly included on our life schedule from the day we were born"
(p. 16).

When life moves toward death as promise and fulfillment, then the aged have a future toward which to look. Life becomes not a waiting for death as the end, but a preparation for the next stage of life. So, life is lived up until the end because the end is not actually the end, but a new beginning.

These latter years bring persons close to the ultimate reality. They move toward the end as new beginning with expectation and with little fear. As they reach toward that which is yet to be, they do not resent the fact that their grip is broken on that to which it was so important to hold. Almost imperceptibly, as they stop grasping for things, they feel that their lives are in the gentle grasp of God, and all is well.

These, then, are basic affirmations of faith that inform every stage of life and inform no less the experience of aging. The creator has fashioned men and women in his own image and has placed a value upon them. That value does not diminish with the onset of age. All persons are flawed by rebellion against God and are incomplete in their own lives, but God in Christ accepts and redeems life at all stages. Thus, no life lived in this faith is ever wasted. Because life in all its stages is a gift, all of life must be a stewardship. There is a peculiar stewardship for the aged to share experience, to give an example of life that has value in itself, and to remind the rest of society what the lasting values and realities are. Finally, death becomes not destruction but fulfillment. The aged move toward it as the God-given future. Therefore, death is accepted as God's gift and so it, too, is transformed.

REFERENCES

Asquith, Glenn H. *Death is all right.* New York: Abingdon Press, 1970.
Comfort, Alex. *A good age.* New York: Crown Publishers, Inc., 1976.
Pearson, Lester B. *Words and occasions.* Toronto: University of Toronto Press, 1970.
Tournier, Paul. *Learn to grow old.* New York: Harper and Row Publishers, 1972.

Chapter 9

WALKING WITHOUT FAINTING
THOMAS C. COOK, SR.

They that wait upon the Lord shall renew their strength; they shall mount up with wings as eagles; they shall run and not be weary; they shall walk and not faint.

Isaiah 40:31

A recent folder from a Christian bookstore lists a number of books written for the elderly. On the front page of the brochure is a picture of an old couple, leaning on one another as they walk along. Beside the picture is their prayer: "Oh God, we can no longer fly like an eagle, or run without being weary. But this is the only time we will be old, show us what to do with these years."

God has shown us what to do with the latter years. Despite much pessimism, there have been people all through the ages who have made the most of the latter years, called by Ecclesiastes the "evil days." They have, through God, shown us what to do with old age: how to walk without fainting.

The evidence is overwhelming that the elderly do not have to be shelved or put out to pasture or be regarded as past their prime, useless, and with nothing to contribute. On the contrary, a full, satisfying, meaningful life can be lived until the very end, by all who choose to "do justly, and to love mercy, and to walk humbly with their God" (Micah 6:8b).

One Who Truly Walked Without Fainting

Let us consider one whose life might show us clearly what to do with our latter years, how to walk without fainting. We first read of Enoch in Genesis 5:21-23: "... and Enoch lived sixty and five years, and begat Methuselah, and Enoch walked with God after he begat Methuselah three hundred years, and begat sons and daughters: and all the days of Enoch were three hundred and sixty

71

five years: and Enoch walked with God and was not; for God took him."

It is interesting to note, in the light of our Social Security system, that when Enoch became sixty-five years old two significant things took place. One, he became a father, and two, he changed his life-style. Instead of applying for his Social Security pension, he sought spiritual security. He began to walk with God. For sixty-five years, we might assume that Enoch merely existed. For the next three hundred years, the implication is that he walked with a purpose.

We must emphasize the fact that Enoch walked *with* God. He did not run ahead of God, nor did he lag behind; he walked with Him. Many of the greatest saints have made the mistake of failing to stay with God. Noah is said to have walked with God, but he got out of step, made a detour, and became shamelessly drunk. Abraham, father of the faithful and friend of God, made a detour into Egypt, that but for God's grace might have proved ruinous. David, the man after God's own heart, made that tragic detour with Bathsheba. His folly plagued him the rest of his days. Always, when we lose step with God and go our own way, we faint. Enoch saw fit to walk with God. How did he do it?

The writer of Hebrews gives us a clue. In chapter eleven of that remarkable book are listed those who through faith achieved greatly for God. Along with Enoch are such stalwarts as Noah, Abraham, Moses, Sarah, Jacob, Joseph and David. Verses 5 and 6 read: "By faith Enoch was translated that he should not see death; and was not found, because God had translated him: for before his translation he had this testimony, that he pleased God. But without faith it is impossible to please Him." One need look no further for an explanation as to how Enoch was able to walk with God. He walked with God because he pleased God, and he pleased God because he had faith in Him.

It is quite plain that nothing pleases God more than our faith in Him, and nothing is more displeasing to Him than our lack of faith. Much of our trouble stems from our failure to please God, and our desperate effort to please ourselves and others. Enoch had this testimony that pleased God. The prophet Amos asks: "Can two walk together, except they be agreed?" (Amos 3:3). Enoch and

God walked together because they were agreed.

Enoch's Walk Paid Off

Obviously, this walk with God afforded Enoch a partnership, one of the basic needs of old age, a time when so much contributes to loneliness: strange surroundings, strange people, strange sounds, strange routines. Loneliness is made more acute by deafness and blindness and separation from family and friends. God has always furnished companionship to those who trust Him. Enoch had a partnership, and unlike the atheist who has no invisible means of support, he, like Moses, "endured as seeing Him who is invisible" (Heb. 11:27).

We, modern Enochs have been given the Comforter, the Holy Spirit, promised by our Lord just before His death. Through the Comforter we walk with Him Who said: "Lo, I am with you always."

One's physical well-being is no small problem for any age. The problem increases with old age. Enoch, we can be sure, was not spared altogether the infirmities of the flesh. He may not have had bifocals or bridges, but he could very well have had baldness, bulges, and bunions. We like to believe he had the stamina of Moses who was "an hundred and twenty years when he died: his eye was not dim, nor his natural force abated" (Deut. 34:7). Then again, Enoch could have been like Jacob, of whom it is written: "The eyes of Israel were dim for age, so that he could not see" (Gen. 45:10), or even like David, who seems to have dreaded old age. Whatever his physical condition, Enoch believed God's promise: "As thy days, so shall thy strength be" (Deut. 33:25).

Where one is to live poses a real problem for all in our day—especially the aged. That problem was solved for Enoch. He was happy wherever he found himself if that was where God wanted him to be. Our address may not even show on a map, but if it is where God has placed us, it is a large place. It may be no more than an obscure country church, a nursing home, a sick-room, but if God wills it, that makes it large and great. We often make the mistake of thinking that all we need in order to be satisfied is a change of environment. We reason that if we can just move into a bigger house, move up a little higher on the social ladder, move to the mountains in summer and south in the winter, all will be well. We blame our failures and unhappiness on heredity and environment. The doctrine of heredity and environment got a severe blow in the Garden of Eden. It will help to remember that Enoch and Abraham had "no continuing city, but we seek one to come" (Heb. 13:14).

Enoch lost no sleep over things. The IRS would not have bothered him. He did not have a high enough income bracket, and he was too honest, nor would he have been on welfare. He may well have prayed: "Give me neither poverty nor riches; feed me with food convenient for me; lest I be full, and say, Who is the Lord?" (Prov. 30:8).

In the last century an American tourist visited the renowned Polish Rabbi Hofetz Chaim. The tourist was amazed to find the Rabbi's home only a simple room, filled with books, a table, and a bench. "Rabbi," he asked, "Where is your furniture?"

"Where is yours?" asked the Rabbi.

"Mine?" asked the puzzled American. "But I'm only a visitor here. I'm only passing through."

"So am I," replied the Rabbi.

Walter Lippmann spoke of "the tyranny of things." Things can tyrannize if not properly gotten or properly handled. Enoch laid "aside every weight" (Heb. 12:1), got rid of all excess baggage, and traveled light. We would do well to follow his example.

It probably never occurred to Enoch that he would ever find the cupboard bare. He walked with a God who could boast: "Every beast of the forest is mine, and the cattle on a thousand hills" (Psa. 50:10). We pride ourselves on our efficiency, forgetting that all our efficiency without God's sufficiency adds up to a miserable deficiency. We would do well to settle down with God now. The day will come when only God will remain. Our bodies, our homes, our bank accounts, our jobs, all these sustain us but temporarily. They shall all one day perish, leaving us with all we ever had really to begin with: God.

Enoch's walk with God makes it clear that quality counts more than quantity; that having life added to our years is far better than having years added to our lives; that we do well not to confuse the means of living with the ends: the things we live with and the things we live for. A recent book bears the title *Life After Life (1975)*, which could be a splendid title for a biography of Enoch. The statement in Hebrews, "It is appointed unto men once to die" (Heb. 9:27) did not apply to Enoch, for the same writer declares, "By faith Enoch was translated that he should not see death; and was not found, because God had translated him" (Heb. 11:5). Just how the journey from earth to heaven was made, we are not told.

The manner in which he made the change is not important. The important thing is that Enoch so walked with God for three hundred earthbound years that he journeyed with Him into eternity. It was as though his life had come full cycle and would forever more "mount up with wings as eagles," no more to "run," "walk," or "faint."

REFERENCE

Moody, Raymond A., Jr. *Life after life.* Atlanta: Mockingbird Books, 1975.

Chapter 10

RELIGIOUS NEEDS OF OLDER PERSONS

Philip S. Brown

O nce an ancient sage peered out upon his world in a vain effort to find fellow humans who might recognize the validity of his personhood in old age. Finding no meaningful response, he turned to his God for help, saying:

> Do not cast me off when old age comes, nor forsake me when my strength fails, when my enemies' rancor bursts upon me and those who watch me whisper together, saying, 'God has forsaken him; after him! sieze him; no one will rescue him.' (Psalm 71:9-11)

The dilemma of the sage is also a modern-day problem for older persons in American society. Having lost many former roles, while facing the onset of chronic diseases and the presence of death, the older adult must zero in on the basic issues of life. The person is not concerned about the long-range goals but has a sense of immediacy. It is a concern for answers to such questions as—

Being — Who am I?
Doing — What is my purpose?
Becoming — Where am I going?

It is to these very issues that religion must address itself, in some unique way, so as to enable persons to express their own humanity. Religion is not a set of beliefs about man, God, and an organization. Religion is a restlessness, an inner drive and need that causes man to seek order and purpose in his life. Unfortunately, the social activism of many religious groups has been centered on the material goods of money, housing, transportation, and medical care. These are needed, but it seems rather obvious that in religion, people are looking for an answer to the non-material issues of life.

Many times the way in which religious groups reveal their pietistic views of aging and God is very demeaning, even in the non-material aspects. A recent church newsletter carried this Prayer for Older People:

> Lord, Thou knowest that I am growing older. Keep me from becoming talkative and possessed with the idea that I must express myself on every subject.
>
> Release me from the craving to straighten out everybody's life.
>
> Keep my mind free from the recital of endless detail. Give me wings to get to the point and then be quiet.
>
> Seal my lips when I am inclined to tell of my aches and pains. They are increasing with the years and my love to speak to them grows sweeter as time goes by.
>
> Make me thoughtful but not nosy; helpful but not bossy. With my vast store of wisdom and experience it does seem a pity not to use it all, but Thou knowest, Lord, that I want a few friends at the end. (Author Unknown)

The basic purpose in religion is to help a person to look beyond himself or herself, to have some view, experience, or realization of transcendence. "Here the person finds that the ultimate task of human consciousness must finally surrender" (Carmondy, 1975). Such an understanding begins with the individual's self-image as known in his or her mental capabilities and capacities. These needs will not be resolved by improving income, housing, transportation, or medical care.

During recent years, social scientists and others have made studies of the religious and/or spiritual needs of older people. A question still being debated is: Do people become more religious in older adulthood? That is, are they more religious when compared to either themselves at a younger age or to the younger generation today? Moberg (1965) and Blazer and Palmore (1976) point out that the answer to this question depends upon the criteria used. If one measures religiosity by church attendance, contributing money and time, adherence to religious doctrine, or having a unique knowledge of the Bible, then older people show a decline in religious involvement. However, if one explores an older person's practice of devotional observance and identity as a religious person, an upsurge in the importance of religion in an older person's life is found.

It is important to note that while physical disabilities, income level, health status, and transportation do have a bearing on the active participation that an older person may take in a religious organization, older people are more concerned about personal relationships, a sense of personal worth before their maker, and how to deal with personal fears, crises, and losses. "It has been demonstrated that older persons tend to seek comfort, not challenge, from their relationship to the church. Those ministers who are more comfort-oriented, not the community activists, enjoy meeting their needs" (Longino & Kitson, 1976).

One implication of this, according to Blazer and Palmore (1976) is that churches need to give special attention to elderly members in order to compensate for a declining level of religious activities, while maximizing the benefits of their religious experience. Sister St. Michael Guinan (1976) highlights this point: "One reason that the emotional shock following retirement is so intense — inside and outside the monastery — is the personality immaturity that besets an affluent society where physiological subsistance is assured, but psychological and spiritual growth find little stimulation."

In an attempt to provide opportunities for personal confrontation with the religious needs of older people, let us review four possible world views held by people, as a means of finding a starting place toward understanding the religious needs of older persons.

The first is the view of the world that states God does not exist. Traditionally, this view is called atheism. The modern-day version of atheism does not debate the issue of the existence of God, but it just makes a proclamation of non-existence. In addition, contemporary atheism has become more humanistic. "Men are truly brothers — not because they are children of a loving God, but because they are alone in a world of unbearable sorrow and suffering" (Strunk, 1968). Human beings are self-made, rootless persons, according to this point of view, whose sameness becomes goodness in light of the awesome terror of the catastrophic threat that continuously holds charge over mankind.

A second view of the world, theism, claims God as creator but not Lord of Life. God does not get involved, because he is removed from the world. God may become involved later on, perhaps, if the right conditions prevail.

The third view of the world places God in a religious compartment of life. God is recognized as creator, sustainer, and savior who is personally involved with his people. However, God is carefully confined to a limited portion of life, world, and the universe. The individual with this belief is a Sunday or Sabbath Day worshiper only.

A fourth view of the world reverses the whole process and sees man, a world, and the universe as a part of God. As the Psalmist wrote:

> Where can I escape from thy spirit?
> Where can I flee from thy presence?
> If I climb up to heaven, thou are there;
> If I make my bed in Sheol, again I find thee.
>
> (Psalm 139:7-8)

A person's world view, though different in conception of God, generally expresses the metaphysical longings within the individual to search out deep and abiding religious needs. As Lance Webb (1965) summarized the condition:

> The big question is not whether we may develop technically a society of abundance and order where all human needs are met, but whether we are capable of the moral and spiritual character required to create and sustain it.
>
> In the personal realm, the question is not for most of us whether we can make a living even with a reasonable amount of luxury, but whether we can find a meaning that transcends the absurdities of boredom, emptiness, lovelessness, and death.

The fourth world view, wherein people see life as operating within the being of God, helps the individual overcome the anxieties about separation and death. It is a source of great comfort that nothing shall or can separate them from the love of God. Death becomes a doorway to a fuller, richer experience with God. The person approaches death with confidence and expectation.

The full impact of such a view becomes rather hard to anticipate because it has a tendency to raise the individual above the mundane problems and occurrences that are normally so important: cultural values, material goods, family relationships, and health needs. The difficulty of comprehending this view is the fact that a unique set of values prevails. However, the new outlook does not exempt the individual from loneliness, sorrow, feelings of uselessness, and other human problems. The person, though, does gain new insight and understanding into all such problems.

The thrust of religion is to help people to move beyond themselves, to experience transcendence, to know who we are, where we come from, and where we are going. The crisis facing modern man is the tendency to understand one's personhood as an entity separate from the past. If a human being operates in such a vacuum, being cut off from God and the insight of one's tradition, then that human being "is a torso without a head, a body without a head, a tree without roots" (Sherwin, 1976).

People are in search of meaning beyond the seeming absurdity of life. Religion can speak to these needs in a unique and supportive way, because the individual is deeply involved with mind, body, and spirit in the process. Older people have a need to move beyond themselves and their other problems, to experience a positive power for a good that is beyond them.

The positive good becomes a creative force to stimulate the individual to respond fully as a human to God. It is not baby cereal with warm milk, but it is a tension that causes the person to use all of his or her current resources to move beyond self. In summary, the religious needs of older persons can be seen as centering in the individual's struggle to experience self-transcendence. Such religious needs seem to be concerned with the basic questions of who am I, what is my purpose, and where am I going?

Religious needs are not static, that is, they cannot be met once and then forgotten. Most major religions have built in the necessity for weekly or daily rites to be enacted by the individuals or participants. Traditionally, the great religions have always separated the spiritual from material needs. However, during the twentieth century, with a greater emphasis upon social action by the religious faiths, the tendency to mix material and spiritual needs has caused organized religions to lose sight of the distinctly religious needs of the person, especially those of the older person.

In looking at world views, one can see only a slight variation in the need of the older person to be on a journey of faith, in search of meanings that transcend the absurdities of retirement, loss of spouse, confinement to a nursing home, or the nearness of one's own death. In reviewing the research on religious needs of older persons, it is clear that older people's participation in religious activities is limited. It is important to understand that older people do often identify themselves as being a religious person. Devotional literature, radio listening, and television viewing are important mediums in the religious growth of an older person. Older people need to have religious groups that will appreciate their tradition, respect their commitments, encourage them to find meaning in the non-activist role, produce meaningful religious broadcasts, and develop a corps of trained visitors to visit the homebound to assist in older person's religious growth needs.

Older persons need the comfort that religious faith can produce. They should not be degraded into feeling that their only religious role is that of "craming for the finals." Old age is a natural part of the life-cycle and has its own distinct religious needs.

REFERENCES

Blazer, D. & Palmore, E. Religion and aging in a longitudinal panel. *The Gerontologist,* 1976, *16,* 83-86.

Carmondy, D. L. Longeran's religious person. *Religion In Life,* 1975, *2,* 223-231.

Guinan, Sr. S. M. Aging and the religious life. *The Gerontologist,* 1972, *12,* 20-21.

Longino, C. F. & Kitson, G. C. Parish clergy and the aged: examining stereo-
types. *Journal of Gerontology,* 1976, *16,* 31-35.
Moberg, D. O. Religiosity in old age. *The Gerontologist,* 1965, *5,* 78-87.
Sherwin, B. L. Journal of a soul: Abraham Joshua Heschel's quest for self
understanding. *Religion In Life,* 1976, *3,* 270-277.
Strunk, O. *The choice called atheism.* Nashville: Abingdon Press, 1968.
Webb, L. *On the edge of the absurd.* Nashville: Abingdon Press, 1965.

Chapter 11

AN AFFIRMATION OF LIFE

Martin Luther King, Sr.

I suppose that I will be making the statement that I am about to make now for the rest of my life, and that is I am a humble man. The Kings are not high and mighty people, we are just humble and down to earth. I came to that through my mother and father, and I taught it to my three children, two of whom have gone to live with God. My daughter is still surviving. Martin Luther King, Jr., was humble, kind, and down to earth. So I want us to be seen that way and we mean it.

I get invitations from all across the country and the world. Often times I have to ask why. In the first place, I am a very practical individual. I try to never get so high that you cannot pick up what I am saying. I was invited to one of our Jewish Synagogues, The Temple, here in Atlanta, as the keynote speaker for their Friday night service recently. I toyed with that invitation for a while. I know what they teach and what they believe, and they do not believe as much in Jesus as we Protestants. I said to my daughter and my daughter-in-law, "I am going but, I don't see how in the world I can speak over there without Jesus."

They laughed, and Coretta said, "Just go on and preach about Jesus, that's all." But we got along very well that night.

I have a message that I am very desperately trying to get across to the world. I would like for you to help me carry it across the world. If we would do this we would have all of our problems licked. We all would really become one people, one church, under God. I am not bitter. I carry no ill will in my heart against any man. I refuse to stoop low enough to hate anybody. *Don't you feel hate.* If anybody could hate, I could be the president of the Hate Society. But I am not going to hate.

I have seen a lot, and with the burden of country boy in the depths of segregation, I have seen a lot and heard a lot. God only

83

knows why I am here today. I remember where my mother had washed and ironed for the white lady and when her son and the little neighbors and I were playing. We were just little boys, and he was just as pure in heart as he could be. My nickname was Mike. He said, "Mike," and then he called the other two boys and said, "let's go up to the house and get a sandwich." We all went on up to the house, and I was the last to enter. The mother opened the front door and they ran in and then she slammed the door in my face. Her little son said, "Mama, that's our friend."

She said, "Well, he'll have to go around the back." That did something to my soul! Just little boys. I went around there. My Mama was ironing in the kitchen.

In a few minutes the lady came and offered me a sandwich and I said, "No, thank you." My mama told me to come in and I said "No, Mama, I'll never come in that house, never. I'm going on home."

She said, "No, go on down and see your uncles and wait until I get there."

I waited for her, and on our way home, I said, "Mama, I am always going to obey you, but I am going to hate white folks."

I stand here to tell you tonight: I hate nobody. I do not intend ever to hate. And, I know why I love every man. I do not hate the man that is supposed to be serving time for taking the life of my son Martin. I do not hate him, I have no ill will against him. They called and asked me if I would protest him being executed, and I said, "I don't believe in capital punishment, but that is a matter for the court. I don't want to be bothered with it." The one that took the life of my wife, I do not hate him. I am serious.

Now don't *you* hate. I do not look as old as I am. I believe that to be because I have no ill will, because I have no hate. I have no ugly face, and I never am going to have it. So, I am every man's brother.

I have a job to do; every day I live and I am going on with my job, going on being every man's brother. So, I love you, every one of you; I hope you love me. Now, I want you to help me carry that across the world. If you do it, you are free. I am free.

I am not worrying about dying. I make no preparation for dying. Any man that dies has failed to live. I am going to fall to sleep one day. This old house of clay is going to give away where it leaks. I will have to move out. But let that old body die, I do not prepare to die.

Thank God for what you have left. No, you cannot do what you did when you were young—never again. But, whatever it is, thank God for what you have left. You, too, have affliction somewhere? You have some hurts, arthritis, bursitis, or all the rest? Thank God for what you have left; that He has given you strength and faith enough to go through with life. I have an ankle that I have to live with the rest of my life. Sometimes it bothers me so much that I cannot go without a cane. I have been in a wheelchair, and I have been on crutches. I have been in pain. It still pains me when I walk too far or stand too long. I can thank God, though, for what I have left. I can finally get where I am going. I may not get there fast, but I can still get there. Thank God that I have that left.

We aged and senior citizens have something else to be very thankful for. Most of us have false teeth. We used to have good teeth and had no tooth ache, had none of our teeth missing. Then they kept on coming out until we lost them all, and we had to buy some teeth. So we do not have those teeth that God gave us, we have bought teeth. But we can still eat. So, thank God you still have some teeth that you can eat with. We were having a testimony meeting not long ago, and different ones were getting up thanking God for what they had faced and one said, "I want to say just a word—I want to thank God for my teeth. You remember, Brother and Sister, the last time you saw me I didn't have no teeth, but I have my teeth now. Thank God for my teeth." Thank God for what you have left.

Working with the aged is a great ministry. The Church has many ministries, but I know of none better than this one: to plan and work hard toward the interests of aged. You will go down the hill soon enough, and we will become the least of these no matter what we have. All of us are beggars, one way or the other. No man lives alone. No man owns himself. He belongs.

Acclamation means committing ourselves wholly to God, and to the spirit of God. I found my hope in God, not in materialistic things. Not in these things that will perish, but in God. People ask me, "How do you take all you take? How do you stand up as you stand up? You are an inspiration to all of us through what you face. How do you do it?" This is simple to answer—I confirmed my faith in God long ago. I hold on Him. He is the source. And, I know He is going to see me through.

I have to sometimes look at that cup that another minister talked about in Harlem. When the Depression was deepest, a mother had just one glass of milk with four or five children to drink from that one glass. He said all the children but one begged to drink and finally one of the children said, "Mama, Mama, how deep can I drink?" Then she measured it off.

Sometimes, when these trials and tribulations hit you, you have to ask God, "Oh, God, how much? How deep must I drink?" So I say occasionally to God, "God how much more must I bear?" I never ask Him why. Because I know He is going to see me through. I have that faith in God.

I am going to wind up down here in this place in this world, and so are you. The aged, and you that are not aged, are going to soon be there. Just keep on living and you will be there. Try your best to live well, so when you get there you will have a happy place to live.

An old doctor lived in the community who was not licensed, he was not school trained. He made his own medicine, carried in his bag, but he got people well. They loved him. He could cure their headaches, and he could cool their temperatures. That old man got people well, with no degree, giving the glory to God. Some people went up in wagons one Saturday to see the old doctor, and he was not home, and they stood there amazed, bothered and disturbed, wondering where the old doctor had gone. An old man came by and they asked him if he knew where the doctor had gone and he said, "Read the sign. He left a sign on his door—read it." And, they began to read the sign. They are going to read your sign and they are going to read mine one day. And you know what the sign said? The old doctor left it there: "Still in business, just moved upstairs."

Section III
SPIRITUAL WELL-BEING IN RELATION TO SELF

Chapter 12

SPIRITUAL WELL-BEING OF THE ELDERLY IN RELATION TO SELF

BETTY J. LETZIG

We cannot ignore the other elements of relationship to community and environment but *self* and *God* cannot be distinguished. How, as persons, we perceive ourselves in relationship to God and our personal faith can affect the relationship to community and environment beyond the effect of both on the person—a triumph over odds.

Paul Tournier (1972) speaks of two turning points in life. The first is from childhood to adulthood; the second is from adulthood to old age. He says: "In the middle of life we must stop to think, to organize our existence with an eye to a still distant future, instead of allowing ourselves to be entirely sucked into the professional and social whirl" (p. 12).

Erickson (1963) emphasizes the stage of ego integrity, a time of readiness to take responsibility for what one's life has been and to become reconciled to one's past as well as to one's future. Tournier (1972) cites Adolf Partmann of Basle, who also speaks to this point: "The man who has not already learned to look for the meaning of his life, is unlikely to be able to organize his old age in a way that will enable him to find it then." (p. 8).

Tournier (1972) also cites Jung, who says, "To refuse to grow old is as foolish as to refuse to leave behind one's life in accordance with the programs appropriate to the morning, since what had great importance then will have very little now, and the truth of the morning will be the error of the evening" (p. 11).

Richard A. Kalish, in his book *Late Adulthood: Perspectives on Human Development* (1975), speaks of the importance of self-esteem and self-concept. Getting older means learning to appreciate yourself. An awareness that some behavior may change, a time for marshalling and utilizing our own resources, an

89

awareness of the human aging process enables each of us to cope more effectively with the aging of those we love, with the aging of our friends and associates, and with the aging that will inevitably come to each of us.

The difficulties that hinder the development of positive attitudes are in our community and our environment and are evident in media presentations, public attitudes, and self-concepts.

In Japan, when the question was asked as to what was the supreme good in their country the answer was, "Our old people."

Lou Harris's poll of attitudes toward the elderly (1975) in our own country was negative among all age groups including the elderly. One hopeful aspect, however, was that even though the elderly felt negatively about elderly people, in general, that was not how they saw themselves.

George Maddox (1974) refers to the tendency of society to categorize people as a sort of "if you've seen one, you've seen them all" attitude—coupled with a casting off "no deposit—no return attitude"—so that the elderly, like bottles, can be drained of their resources and then discarded. We have recently begun to recognize and talk of this as "agism" as it is evident in early lay-offs, discrimination in employment, and forced retirement.

Definitions of "successful aging" have tended to emphasize the importance of *self-esteem* and *self-concept.* Successful aging perhaps may be encouraged by learning something about what it means to become elderly, effectively coping with changes in order to live as much as possible as one wishes.

Kalish has identified basic needs of the elderly as essentially the same as those of all other age groups: the need to have physiological and safety needs met, the need to feel loved so self-esteem can be maintained, the need to be challenged, the need to be able to realize one's own potential, and the need for dignity—as important in old age as in youth—in the dying process as in the rest of life (Kalish, 1975).

Dr. Paul Maves (see Chapter 6 in this book), in a personal communication, shared some of his thinking on this subject:

Spiritual well-being of self can be thought of in terms of qualities of courage, gallantry, human commitment, and relationships. It requires a vision of reality which enables us to put the struggle to be something utterly other than what we are into proper perspective—a vision that we do not have to achieve value but that we have value because we are human. It requires the understanding that life is a pilgrimage rather than a place to stand, a pilgrimage that leads beyond our own histories, a process in which we are caught up and carried along with our companions, a journey to be completed beyond time.

Ultimately, it is a matter of living differently but not less. In 1945, General Douglas MacArthur said that you do not get old from living a particular number of years, you get old because you have deserted your ideals. Years will wrinkle your skin, renouncing your ideals wrinkles your soul. Worry, doubt, fear, and despair are the enemies that slowly bring us down to the ground and turn us to dust before we die.

Paul Tournier (1972) speaks of the second career as a goal, a mission. It is an opportunity for work that is more social, that expresses more love of people, that is not an escape but a presence in the world, a time to give up giving orders. It is a time characterized by spontaneity and a time to give up being a leader even if remaining an advisor. It is a continuing recognition that God has a plan for every person at every moment.

REFERENCES

Erikson, E. H. *Childhood and society.* New York: Norton, 1963.

Harris, L. *To be old in America.* Washington, D.C.: National Council on Aging, 1975.

Kalish, R. A. *Late adulthood: Perspectives on human development.* Monterey, California: Brooks/Cole Publishing Co., 1975.

Maddox, G. & Pfeiffer, E. (Eds.). *Successful aging—a conference report.* Durham, N.C.: Duke University Press, 1974.

Partmann, A., cited in Tournier, P. *Learn to grow old.* New York: Harper & Row, 1972.

Tournier, P. *Learn to grow old.* New York: Harper & Row, 1972.

Chapter 13

PERSONAL AND INSTITUTIONALIZED RELIGIOSITY OF THE ELDERLY

Constance L. Brennan and Leo E. Missinne

A ttempting to investigate the possible relationship between religiosity and aging presents several obstacles to researchers. The difficulty in delineating the concept of religion as well as the many variations in individual definitions and personal meanings makes research arduous. Further, because persons age in various ways, the relationship between religiosity and aging is particularly elusive. The project summarized here sought to determine how important the individual sees religion as being in his life, as well as any perceived changes in belief or participation. This study of personal religiosity was directed toward answering several specific questions with regard to changes that may occur in the individual's religious feelings as he ages.

A hypothesis regarding personal religiosity may be stated: Persons who are religiously oriented in youth or young adulthood will tend to remain religiously oriented throughout later life, although the quality of personal religiosity may change and develop throughout the lifespan. Conversely, persons who are not religiously oriented in the younger years will tend to remain non-religious in later life.

Related Studies

In reviewing previous research for support or refutation of this hypothesis, the five dimensions of religiosity postulated by Glock (1962) were used. Stated briefly, these dimensions are: (1) the experiential, or the degree to which religion elicits an emotional response from its adherents; (2) the ideological, or the beliefs and doctrines that are held by the individual; (3) the ritualistic, or the

activities advocated by formal religions, including church attendance and both public and private formal prayer; (4) the
intellectual, or the extent to which individuals are knowledge-
able regarding their faith and its teachings; and (5) the consequential, or the effects of religiosity on the individual's everyday
life.

Regarding the experiential aspects of religion, Swenson (1967)
reported that the highest proportion of those who had experienced some very unusual religious experiences was in the seventy
and over age group, who also reported "more often" feeling very
religious. In three additional studies (Marshall and Oden, 1962;
Jeffers and Nichols, 1961; Lloyd, 1955), people reported that
religion had become more important to them as they aged, rather
than the reverse. However, Nila Covalt (1960) found no evidence
to support the idea that people turn to religion as they grow older.

Research into the ideological dimension of religion has
primarily been done through surveys. The 1966 Catholic Digest
Survey indicated that 86 percent of those aged sixty-five and over
were certain that there is a God, with less respondents being
certain in each of the younger age groups (Riley and Foner, 1968).
Similar results were found concerning a belief in immortality, the
importance of religion, and in conservative Christian doctrine
such as biblical miracles, the devil, and the deity of Jesus. In
surveys measuring all of these beliefs, older respondents had a
higher proportion of believing responses than did persons in
younger age groups.

The ritualistic dimension of religion may be easier to study
than others since religious practices such as church attendance
and public prayer may be readily observed. In his review of
research, Moberg (1965) found that the elderly, as well as other
groups, participate more in church organizations than in all
other forms of social activities combined. Most of the research in
the area of church attendance indicates that participation remains fairly stable from early adulthood through the mid sixties.
After this, church attendance often declines, with the most often
reported reasons being poor health, lack of transportation, or
lack of finances. Women participate somewhat more than men,
and church membership is often the last social affiliation to be

given up. Some surveys have indicated that church participation increases with age, though these are in the minority.

The intellectual dimension of religion seems to have been the most neglected by researchers. Davidson (1969) found that knowledge about church history and teachings was greatest in those aged sixty and over. These persons were also more reluctant to challenge their church's teachings. In looking at age differences in religious knowledge, it is well to remember that teaching methods have been modified over the years, and this may affect the amount of knowledge retained.

Some studies (Moberg 1965) have shown that persons active in church organizations are more frequently active in other groups than are non-church members. This may reflect religious attitudes or, as Moberg suggests, may be because association with people in one area often leads to knowledge of and interest in other groups. This may also reflect personality differences between extroverted joiners and the more introverted non-joiners.

Religious beliefs and faith in God have helped disorganized patients to overcome grief and depression (Wolff, 1959) and illustrate the consequential aspect of religion in everyday life. Apparently, religious attitudes also significantly influence the individual's attitudes toward death and dying (Swenson, 1961; Jeffers, Nichols, and Eisdorfer, 1961). Those who viewed death positively used religious beliefs to support their opinions; however, those who denied or feared death also demonstrated an absence of religious terminology. Feifel (1959) found that non-religious persons not only had these concerns but also often worried about their destiny—punishment or reward—after death.

From the research cited, some of which is contradictory and inconclusive, there is clearly a need for further investigation into the relationship between religiosity and aging. Because most of the studies have been cross-sectional, the differences attributed to age may reflect societal and cultural changes as well. To control for such variables and obtain more conclusive data will require more longitudinal research. Such research is difficult to conduct because of the time and expense involved. The present study, though not longitudinal, is an attempt to provide additional data concerning the relationship between religiosity and aging. As this relationship becomes clearer, planners of religious programs will hopefully be able to meet the spiritual needs of the elderly more effectively.

The primary objective of the research was to determine how older persons in a Midwestern community view their religious development throughout adulthood. Elderly subjects were asked to compare their current religious feelings and participation with those of earlier adulthood.

Methodology and Results

A total of ninety-two persons, ranging in age from fifty-nine to ninety-three years, were asked to respond to a brief questionnaire concerning religious feelings and participation as they are now and as they are remembered from earlier adulthood. Three groups of respondents were participants in congregate meal sites. All were in good health, living independently in the community. Economically, these subjects were middle or low income. The fourth group consisted of twelve residents of a retirement village. While these subjects were somewhat better-off financially, they were similar to the other respondents in terms of health and independent living. The total sample of ninety-two subjects contained thirty-four males and fifty-eight females.

Respondents were asked to give their self-views in terms of religiosity. Questions were worded to ask for both the present view as well as how they saw themselves in early adulthood. It is recognized that such reliance on personal memory has limitations regarding validity. However, the primary purpose of the study was to determine if older persons themselves felt that they had become more religious as they aged.

In addition to the questionnaire used, participants were encouraged to add personal comments, and interviews were conducted with some persons who did not wish to answer the questionnaire. Because there were no significant differences among the four groups, responses were combined into one sample. The results from the survey are summarized in Table 13-I.

Table 13-I
Responses to a Religious Questionnaire by a Sample of Elderly

Question	YES		NO	
	Number	Percent	Number	Percent
Do you believe in God?	91	99	1	1
Have you always?	91	99	1	1
Do you consider yourself a religious person?	84	91	8	9
Have you always?	66	72	26	28
Do you attend church or temple regularly?	67	73	25	27
Have you always?	68	74	24	26
Do you believe in an afterlife?	86	93	6	7
Have you always?	84	91	6	7
Do you belong to one or more church related organizations?	53	59	37	40
Have you always?	64	72	25	27
Do you feel your clergy cares about you as a person?	76	96	3	4
Do you pray or meditate regularly?	74	83	15	17
Have you always?	48	68	23	32
Is prayer beneficial to you personally?	79	93	6	7
Do you feel accepted by the members of your church?	83	93	6	7
Have you always?	58	83	12	17

$N = 92$

Of the total sample, 91 percent considered themselves to be religious, and 72 percent felt they had been religious throughout adulthood. Eighteen persons (20%) had begun to feel religious during adulthood, ranging in age from sixteen to sixty-five years. Only three persons (3%) had begun to feel religious after age fifty-five. One individual reported becoming less religious after reaching adulthood.

Similar proportions of positive responses were obtained from other questions. Nearly all subjects (99%) believed in God, believed in an afterlife (93%), felt accepted by church members (93%), felt the clergy cared about them (96%), prayed regularly (83%), and felt that prayer was beneficial to them (93%). While there were some persons who had not always held their current beliefs and attitudes, the percentage of those who had changed their feelings was generally small, less than 10 percent. Two exceptions to this were those who had always prayed regularly. While 93 percent of the individuals now felt accepted by church members, only 83 percent had always felt this way. There was no pattern in the ages when they had felt either more or less accepted. At the time of the survey, 83 percent of the sample prayed regularly, but only 68 percent reported that they had always done so. Those who had begun to pray regularly during the adult years had started at various ages, ranging from twenty to fifty-five years.

The lowest proportion of positive responses was in answer to questions related to church attendance and participation in church groups. Though the individuals were living independently, 25 percent did not attend church regularly. The most common reasons given for ceasing attendance were poor health, difficulty in getting around, and lack of transportation.

Each subject was asked to select one of four adjectives that best described him in the present. The four words presented were happy, sad, confused, content. The vast majority of this sample were either happy (39%) or content (49%). Another 5 percent said they felt confused; 5 percent were sad, and 2 percent felt that none of the words were appropriate.

Finally, subjects were asked to list the three most important things in their lives at this time. Religion (and religiously related items), good health, and family were the three most frequent responses.

Implications

The results of this survey tend to support the hypothesis that religious feelings and activities remain fairly constant throughout adult life. The number of persons who reported changing their religious attitudes after reaching adulthood was quite small in most cases. Those changes that were reported showed no correlation with age. That is, where there was change, the incidence of change was as frequent in young adulthood as in the later years. Further, there was no apparent relationship between the individual's self-description and degree of religiosity. Most of the subjects were happy or content, but those who were confused or sad were equally likely to consider themselves to be religious.

In relative importance, religion was second in number of responses to good health, and it was tied with family. If, however, all responses related to religion were interpreted as religious, the importance of religion moves ahead of both family and good health. In either event, religion seems to be one of the important items in the lives of older persons.

This study, despite its limitations, tends to provide similar results to other research discussed earlier. If any tentative conclusion can be drawn from this data it is that just as all persons do not age physically in the same manner, neither do all persons perceive and practice religion in•the same way. Based on the present study, it is impossible to make any conclusive statement regarding the value of religion in helping people adjust to aging. Those who considered religion to be very important expressed the belief that their religiosity did in fact help them to face the difficulties of later life. However, many of them also expressed the belief that religion had been beneficial to them throughout life, not only as they had grown old. This again seems to support the hypothesis that the degree of religiosity is primarily related to the way in which it is perceived and the degree to which the individual develops religious attitudes throughout the lifespan, rather than being related to aging per se.

REFERENCES

Covalt, N.K. The meaning of religion to older people. *Geriatrics*, 1960, *15*, 658-664.

Davidson, J. Religious involvement and middle age. *Sociological Symposium*, 1969, *3*, 31-45.

Feifel, H. (Ed.). *The meaning of death.* New York: McGraw-Hill, 1959.

Glock, C.Y. On the study of religious commitment. *Religious Education*, 1962, *57*, 98-110.

Jeffers, F.C., & Nichols, C.R. The relationship of activities and attitudes to physical well-being in older people. *Journal of Gerontology*, 1961, *16*, 67-70.

Jeffers, F.C., Nichols, C.R., & Eisdorfer, C. Attitudes of older persons toward death: A preliminary study. *Journal of Gerontology*, 1961, *16*, 53-56.

Lloyd, R.G. Social and personal adjustment of retired persons. *Sociology and Social Research*, 1955, *39*, 312-316.

Marshall, H., & Oden, M.H. The status of the mature gifted individual as a basis for evaluation of the aging process. *The Gerontologist*, 1962, *2*, 201-206.

Moberg, D.O. Religiosity in old age. *The Gerontologist*, 1965, *5* (No. 2), 78-87, 111-112.

Moberg, D.O. *Spiritual well-being: Background paper prepared for the White House Conference on Aging*, Washington, D.C.: U.S. Government Printing Office, 1971.

Riley, M.W., & Foner, A. *Aging and society, Vol. I: An inventory of research findings.* New York: Russell Sage Foundation, 1968.

Swenson, W.M. Attitudes toward death in an aged population. *Journal of Gerontology*, 1961, *16*, 49-52.

Wolff, K. Group psychotherapy with geriatric patients in a state hospital setting: Results of a three year study. *Group Psychotherapy*, 1959, *12*, 218-222.

Chapter 14

LIFE REVIEW:
A PASTORAL COUNSELING TECHNIQUE
Bruce J. Horacek

There are a number of ways in which churches and individual ministers can work with and provide services for older people. These include such activities as providing worship services geared to the special needs of older persons; offering religious education programs such as prayer groups and Bible studies; providing such pastoral care services as counseling, chaplaincy services, and information and referral; providing opportunities and financial support for senior citizen clubs, retreats, educational programs, low income retirement housing, and advocacy groups; and providing opportunities for older people to offer their special skills, such as serving as parish leaders, as foster grandparents, and performing such services as friendly visitors, telephone reassurance volunteers, and teaching aides in schools.

One very effective counseling tool for use by ministers with older people is a technique developed by Dr. Robert N. Butler, psychiatrist, gerontologist, and the first Director of the National Institute on Aging. In 1963, Butler argued that the older person is prone to an inner, mental experience of reviewing his life. Butler further postulated that this life review is a universal experience shared by all older people, granted differing intensities and results. He reached this conclusion after observing older persons in clinical as well as research settings, and since that time, he and his colleague, Myrna Lewis, a social worker and psychotherapist, have experimented with the use of life review in individual and group psychotherapy sessions.

This chapter will explore a number of issues involving the concept of life review, including what the life review is, as well as the objectives, techniques, and expectations of life review therapy. Then, the spiritual or religious implications of this technique will be explored. Finally, we will attempt to answer the question: Could this be an effective counseling tool for use by pastors and ministers?

What Is Life Review?

As indicated, Butler argues that life review is a prominent developmental occurrence in the lives of older people. This mental process is usually brought about by the realization of impending death (Butler, 1961; Butler, 1963; Butler and Lewis, 1973; Lewis and Butler, 1974; Butler, 1975). As a person begins to realize that he is mortal, he becomes vulnerable to a mental process characterized by a return to consciousness of events from the past. More often than not, unresolved conflicts from the past will play a key role in this form of review. The goal of life review is to identify the areas of conflict and concern, along with the accompanying fear or guilt, and to eventually resolve these conflicts bringing about a reintegration within the person's consciousness. If such resolution does take place, it will positively contribute to a person's candor, serenity, and wisdom. If such a resolution is not reached, then the process of life review can lead to or exacerbate certain late-life mental disorders, especially depression (Butler, 1963).

Life review as a process usually happens spontaneously. Some persons are fully aware of the process as it is taking place, and therefore consciously aid the process; others are either partially or totally unaware of why events from the past now occupy their thoughts. Furthermore, the experience of life review can differ from person to person, ranging from occasional reminiscing and mild nostalgia to an obsessive preoccupation with past events (Lewis and Butler, 1974). If the process of reintegrating and reorganizing one's life is not completed prior to death, the individual may well suffer severe guilt, anxiety, and despair. In extreme situations the person who has an unsuccessful life review may be suicidal (Butler, 1963).

How does one know when another person is experiencing the life review process? Life review can take the form of sporadic reminiscing and storytelling. In time, this retelling of past experiences may become more frequent, including much repetition, and the person may repeat his life history to anyone willing to listen. Life review may manifest itself in the older person's dreams and nightmares as well as in daydreams and fantasies. These thoughts might include highly symbolic manifestations of past events along with death images. Another common expression of the life review process is mirror-gazing. A person may either praise or angrily scold his mirror image for past deeds or omissions (Butler, 1963).

At this point a special note of caution must be expressed. Butler and Lewis (Butler, 1963; Lewis and Butler, 1974) observe that there is a tendency among professionals to associate reminiscence and repetition with mental disorders found among the institutionalized aged. While the life review may include psychopathological manifestations, nevertheless, Butler considers the basic process to be a normal one. Furthermore, even in the case of repetition and emphasis on the past in brain damaged persons, resolution of underlying conflicts can often be accomplished.

Another cautionary note should be sounded. Since the life review process involves reminiscence, repetition, and a preoccupation with the past, it might be seen as supporting the long-standing stereotype that older people spend most of their time thinking and talking about the past. As recent research has shown (Cameron, 1972, Giambra, 1977), there is little evidence to support the contention that there is a greater tendency for the elderly to reminisce about the distant past than younger people. As Butler (1963) points out, people of all ages review their past on various occasions, especially when faced with certain life crises that precipitate questions of self-identity. Such events as marriage, entering college, graduation, death of a spouse, retirement, or impending death may explain a preoccupation with past events. The life review in older people is most often associated with the life crisis of impending death or the awareness of the short amount of time left to live. Life reviewing for older people takes on a special intensity because of the realization that the present may be the last opportunity to find meaning in life or to resolve past conflicts.

Life Review Therapy

Since Butler states that life review is a natural, universal experience shared by all older people, the question arises as to what role a professional might have in this process. According to Lewis and Butler (1974), the purpose of professional intervention into the life review process is to enhance it, make it more deliberate, conscious, and productive for the older person.

With these objectives in mind, Butler and Lewis have used life review therapy in both individual and group psychotherapy. Furthermore, they have devised several techniques that aid the life review, specifically in evoking memory. Examples of these techniques follow:

1. Using written or taped autobiographies usually opens the door to further communication between the older people and the professional. Omissions and conflicts are examined, and family members often become involved in this process.
2. Pilgrimages, encouraging the person to travel to locations where important events took place during youth and the adult years, serve to unlock numerous memories and conflicts.
3. Attending family, school, or church reunions can be beneficial in examining changes that have taken place over the life cycle.
4. Tracing family lineage can be a very useful tool in enabling an older person to be able to gain a sense of perspective in the continuity of generations of family members.
5. Summation of life work enables those whose work was especially important to them to see meaning in their lives. This technique is particularly useful for those who have no children.
6. Collecting scrapbooks, letters, photographs, and other memorabilia (some people begin to organize such items in old age, while some have done this all their lives) is especially useful in provoking emotions attached to persons, events, and things.

These are just a few examples of the techniques professionals can use to aid older persons in making the life review process more deliberate and productive. Each technique can offer a wealth of material. Important to the whole life review process is the principle of respect; the life review is something the individual initiates and not the professional. Care must be taken to allow the person to proceed at his own pace and to come to his own conclusions. The professional serves as an aid to this process, not as a judge. Meaning in life and resolution of conflicts must be worked out by the individual, not by the professional.

Spiritual Implications of Life Review

The spiritual or religious implications of the life review process become obvious when one examines the goals, expectations, and emotions surrounding this technique. In referring to the outcome of life review, Lewis and Butler state: "All the truly significant emotional options remain available until the moment of death—love, hate reconciliation, self-assertion, and self-esteem" (1974, p. 169). This points to life review as a very active process involving a person who is capable of change and development at every stage of the life cycle. While life review involves looking at the past, the emphasis is on the present: a quest for meaning, for reconciliation, for identity. The concept of life review is an excellent expression of the Judeo-Christian belief that each man is made in the image of God. Each individual possesses worth and dignity; every stage of life, including old age, has intrinsic value and the potential for growth and development.

One of the central tenets of the life review is that the process involves unresolved conflicts and the attempt to deal with and reintegrate them within the personality. This is the essence of the Christian theme of reconciliation. Life review offers an opportunity to understand and accept personal weaknesses and past misdeeds and to take responsibility for our actions. There is the chance to resolve longstanding conflicts, to restore relationships with a spouse, children, relatives, and friends. In restoring relationships, the older person might manifest hitherto unknown personality characteristics and in the process encourage a new intimacy with those around him.

If the life review process is successful, fear of death and dissolution may be lessened. If life is seen as meaningful, if a person's life is seen as worthwhile, then the person can face death as well as the rest of his life. In this context Butler (1963) refers to Erik Erikson's (1963) stages of life, in particular that ego identity is a lifelong development. If a person is able to come to a basic acceptance of his or her life as being appropriate and meaningful, then death loses its sting. This is the stage of ego integrity. If the life review is unsuccessful, conflicts are not resolved, and life is seen as being meaningless and despair or fear of death takes over.

If a person reaches the stage of ego integrity through life reviewing, the future assumes less importance than the present. The older person can be free to enjoy what Lewis and Butler (1974) call "elementality," the ability to experience and enjoy people, nature, love, humor, wisdom, and beauty, as well as a comfortable acceptance of life and the universe. Abraham Heschel, in his address to the 1961 White House Conference on Aging, described this experience the "sense of significant being," a thing of the spirit, "the cry for such relatedness which gains intensity with old age . . . a cry for a referent that transcends personal existence" (1971, p. 34).

These are but a few of the spiritual overtones of the life review process: growth, change, reconciliation, intimacy, ego integrity, a sense of significant being. Heschel described well what could be called the spiritual premise underlying life review. He suggested that "Man's potential for change and growth is much greater than we are willing to admit, and that old age be regarded not as the age of stagnation but as the age of opportunities for inner growth" (1971, p. 34).

Life Review and Pastoral Counseling

Could life review therapy be a useful counseling technique for ministers and pastors? When describing life review therapy, Lewis and Butler (1974) classify it as a psychotherapeutic technique. Consequently, they recommend this tool first to those who might have training in psychotherapy, including psychiatrists, psychologists, social workers, psychiatric nurses, and other professionals. Obviously then, pastors, chaplains, and ministers who are trained in the art of psychotherapy might find life review to be a useful counseling tool. Life review therapy could be used with individuals as well as with groups of older persons or in age-integrated settings.

In addition to those trained in the use of psychotherapy, Butler and Lewis also state that others can aid older people in the process. Therefore, it seems reasonable to conclude that any pastor or minister involved in counseling older persons could benefit from understanding this technique. Further, pastors having counseling experience with older people may already be intrinsically aware of many of the dynamics of the life review process.

Lewis and Butler (1974) indicate that the most introspective part of the life review takes place while persons are in their sixties, and begins to recede in the seventies and eighties. The suggestion here is that perhaps most older people going through this process eventually enter Erikson's developmental stage of ego integrity manifesting candor, serenity, and wisdom. Butler and Lewis also state that life review might also be effective in dealing with older persons suffering from brain damage in terms of helping to reduce the depression and anxiety often accompanying brain damage.

The emphasis throughout this chapter has been on how professionals can aid older adults in the process of life reviewing. We should also note that persons who serve older people in this process are also being served. As Lewis and Butler (1974) suggest, those who aid others with the life review receive in return the benefits of a rich supply of information including "A personal sense of life's flow from birth through death, personal solutions for encountering grief and loss regarding old age and death, and models for growing older and for creating meaningful lives" (p. 173).

REFERENCES

Butler, R.N. The life review: an interpretation of reminiscence in the aged. *Psychiatry*, 1963, *24*, 65-76.

Butler, R.N. Re-awakening interests. *Nursing Home,* Journal of the American Nursing Home Association, 1961, *10,* 8-19.

Butler, R.N. *Why survive? Being old in America.* New York: Harper and Row, 1975.

Butler, R.N., & Lewis, M.I. *Aging and mental health.* Saint Louis: The C. V. Mosby Company, 1973.

Cameron, P. The generation gap: Time orientation. *Gerontologist,* 1972, *12,* 117-119.

Erickson, E.H. *Childhood and Society.* New York: W.W. Norton and Company, 1963.

Giambra, L.M. Daydreaming about the past: The time setting of spontaneous thought intrusions. *Gerontologist,* 1977, *17,* 35-38.

Heschel, A.J. To grow in wisdom. *Christian Ministry,* March, 1971, 31-37.

Lewis, M.I., & Butler, R.N. Life-review therapy: Putting memories to work in individual and group psycho-therapy. *Geriatrics,* November, 1974, 165-173.

Chapter 15

CREATIVE TRANSFORMATION AND THE THEOLOGICAL RESOURCES FOR LONELINESS

WILLIAM A. MCCREARY

The condition of loneliness is a pervasive one in our socio-cultural context. To be human is to experience loneliness. It is a natural dimension of the agony and the ecstasy of our human pilgrimage as interrelational and interdependent beings. Deep within each of us are the existential longings for contact, communication, and companionship. We long for a quality of acceptance, support, and tenderness. We are creatures born for responsive reciprocity and love. Loneliness, however, is the painful and often searing experience that happens as a result of the partial or total dissatisfaction of such longings. If loneliness is so pervasive within our human community, so fundamentally common to our human condition, why does it strike us as so unnatural? If loneliness is a part of the price we pay for being human, why have only a handful of psychiatrists, psychologists, sociologists, and theologians given such little attention to its occcurrence?

Two partial answers emerge in relationship to these kinds of questions. First, the problem of definition is itself difficult. It is made problematic because there are many varied dimensions to its occurrence. For example, many persons equate the experience of *being lonely* with the experience of *being alone*. Would we not agree that every creative endeavor requires a certain dimension of solitude? Would we also not agree that for creative living to occur there need to be times when we are alone with ourselves? In the New Testament, for example, we read that Jesus often withdrew from the crowds to be creatively alone. Throughout history, persons skilled in the art of living have recognized the value of solitude for reflection, rededication, recommitment, and renewal.

Indeed, "to be still and know God" has been a foundational insight into the religious quest for meaning, morale, and motivation. Thus, solitude may well serve to transform our loneliness, but it is not synonymous with it.

A second matter regarding the study of loneliness is revealed in the negative psychological disposition most people commonly hold toward it. Frieda Fromm Reichmann (1959) states in her study on loneliness that it is "such a painful, frightening experience that people will do practically everything to avoid it" (p. 10). Patterns of denial and evasion make it difficult not only to gather information about this particular condition of our humanness but also serve to frustrate meaningful interpretation of it.

The question remains: what exactly do we mean by loneliness? Potthoff (1976) provides a generic definition of loneliness, stating that "Loneliness is the experience of not being meaningfully related." This can be expanded to include "not being meaningfully related" either to oneself, to significant others, to the good earth, or ultimately to God. Though this definition does not clearly delineate the type of loneliness, for example, emotional and social isolation, it does provide us with a working definition for our purposes.

There are many dimensions to the condition of loneliness. Some of these are externally conditioned. A person who is suffering a terminal illness knows the loneliness of a hospital bed. Persons who are physically immobilized or shut-off from a wider participation in life and its becoming know the condition of "not being meaningfully related." Shut-ins know the experience of loneliness. From this perspective, one's world often seems to shrink and close in upon one's self. One begins to wonder: "Is there any world beyond these walls?"

Not all forms of loneliness are externally conditioned. Indeed, some dimensions of loneliness may happen within a socially active context. Persons who experience the absence of meaningful relationships within a social context may experience emotional isolation. In this form, significant emotional bonds are absent by virtue of either death, alienation, or rejection. Loneliness of this type may be historically real (as in the case of the neurotic's fear of personal rejection). Often, emotional isolation is a form of loneliness that is self-chosen and self-sustained. However, let us not depreciate or rationalize the real pain of loneliness that attends such experiences, self-chosen or not. As Weiss (1973) says:

> No matter how much those who are lonely would like to shake it off, no matter how much they may berate themselves for permitting it to overcome them, they find themselves possessed by it. No matter how devotedly they may count their other blessings, no matter how determined they may be to put their minds to other things, the loneliness remains, an almost eerie affliction of their spirits. (p. 13)

Loneliness is therefore both internally and externally conditioned. It involves a variety of forms but is most commonly experienced as the absence of some particular and meaningful provision for relational identity, either socially or emotionally defined. In general, it can be said to be the experience of not being meaningfully related. Ultimately, the experience of loneliness involves our relationship to God.

As its best, religion serves to significantly relate persons to the wholeness of life in its dynamic, relational, and processive becoming. It seeks to provide a vision of greatness within and through which one can meaningfully locate himself in the process of creativity. Great religions affirm that we are not alone as creatures of existence but that we are fundamentally related to all that participates in life through God. Gordon Allport (1950) wrote, "Religion is the audacious bid (one) makes to bind (oneself) to creation and to the Creator. It is the ultimate attempt to enlarge and complete (one's) own personality by finding the supreme context in which (one) rightly belongs" (p. 142). Hence, religion can be a creative resource for understanding and addressing the problem of loneliness. It may also contribute to one's existential estrangement and loneliness by legitimizing patterns of alienation (Berger, 1969).

Fundamentally, religion is theologically concerned with the question of creative transformation. Weiman (1963) states the issue most clearly when he asks: "What operates in human life with such character and power that it will transform man as he cannot transform himself, saving him from evil and leading him to the best life can ever reach, provided he meet the required conditions (of faith, confession, repentance and love)?" (p. 3).

From this perspective, God is seen as creatively present and intimately involved in a process of individuation and becoming. Such a process is relational in character and dynamic in fact. God is responsively involved in our existential condition, entering into the suffering sighs of creation itself. The dramatic events of both Sinai and Golgotha provide vivid testimonies to God's historical involvements. To suffer is to be affected. Thus, God's own creative evolution is affected in part by our own (Whitehead, 1929). This is a foundational insight for what Buber (1970) described as the "I-Thou" encounter.

The awareness of God's transforming presence through the suffering sighs of creativity itself is basic to the idea of religion. From this perspective, the psalmist could pray: "Yea, though I walk through the valley of the shadow of death, I will fear no evil, for Thou art with me; Thy rod and thy staff, they comfort me" (Psalm 23:4). It is in this light too that loneliness can be most creatively considered.

This foundational insight involves four subevents in the process of its creative transformation of the human character into a more richly inclusively whole. According to Weiman (1946):

> The four subevents are: an emerging awareness of qualitative meaning derived from other persons through communication; integrating these new meanings with others previously acquired; expanding the richness of quality in the appreciable world by enlarging its meaning; deepening the community among those who participate in this total creative event of intercommunication. (p. 58)

None of us lives unto himself alone, and none of us dies unto himself alone. Religion not only functions to provide us with a frame of reference in which we can locate ourselves and give meaning to our lives; it not only functions to help us interpret life through rituals and rites; but it also provides us with a meaningful community of faith. We are related to a tradition and to a community of persons who honestly care for and about us. The church and synagogue are essential to our religious maturation and spiritual well-being.

Thus, the creative transformation of our loneliness comes through God's grace to transform us as we cannot transform ourselves through the "I-Thou" encounter, which makes for wholeness.

The darkest nights of the soul's loneliness provide the potential for creative transformation and faith commitments to the source of life itself, God. Such periods of darkness may, if entered into fully, enable us to say "Yes" to God, growing creatively in His way, to say "Yes" to community in each new day, and to say "Yes" to oneself through the sustained expectations of what life together can mean and become.

Loneliness is but one dimension of the human condition affected by that power that can transform our isolation and fragmentation in ways we ourselves cannot realize. We confess with the Psalmist: "It is God who has made us and not ourselves." Indeed, the creative process that deepens and completes our wholeness as persons alive to the fullness of our environment, community, self, and God continues to command and summon our religious and spiritual commitment to life and its creative becoming.

REFERENCES

Allport, G. *The individual and his religion.* New York: Macmillan Company, 1950.

Berger, P. *The sacred canopy.* New York: Anchor Books, 1969.

Buber, M. *I and thou.* New York: Charles Scribner's Sons, 1970.

Potthoff, H. H. *Loneliness: understanding and dealing with it.* Nashville: Abingdon, 1976.

Reichman, F. F. Loneliness. *Psychiatry,* 1959, *21,* 1-10.

Weiss, R. S. *Loneliness: the experience of emotional and social isolation.* Massachusetts: MIT Press, 1958.

Whitehead, A. N. *Process and reality.* New York: The Macmillan Company, 1929.

Weiman, H. N. *The source of human good.* Carbondale: Southern Illinois University Press, 1946.

Weiman, H. N. Intellectual autobiography. In R. W. Bretall (Ed.) *The empirical theology of Henry Nelson Weiman.* Carbondale: Southern Illinois University Press, 1963.

THE AGED, THE JUDEO-CHRISTIAN ETHIC, AND MISUSE OF ILLNESS FOR DEPENDENCY NEEDS

MICHAEL B. MILLER AND FREDRICK J. SCHUMACHER

Clinicians have often been confronted with the clinical paradox in which aged patients who suffer from essentially similar conditions are able to perform the activities of daily living (ADL) at substantially different levels. Patients, for example, who are disabled with rheumatoid arthritis, hemiplegia, or another disease entity, when compared to others who have virtually identical conditions, may differ widely, from being capable of self care to requiring total nursing care at a wheelchair level. Patients presenting no increment of recurrent physical disease may demonstrate, to a substantial degree, intermittent variations in their capacity to perform the activities of daily living.

In medical practice, those patients who appear to be underachievers are often described as "poorly motivated" or in pursuit of "secondary gains" of disability. The intrinsic nature of the basis for such patient underachievement is seldom analyzed or identified. When attempts are made to identify the basis for poor patient performance of ADL, clinical investigation usually terminates with a description of an obvious emotional level of the patient: "patient is depressed," "is anxious," or "has little incentive."

The present study examines the intermingled social, psychological, somatic, and cultural foundations of patient behavior relative to the ability to perform the activities of daily living, with a special focus on the disabled, institutionalized, ill aged.

The comments of Ellis (1975) and Pellegrino (1973) pertaining to students of human and societal behavior identify the core of a too often unexplored clinical experience. Ellis (1975) noted:

The life style of the patient is dependent on the human values held by him. If begun early, alterations of a harmful life style can prevent the development of many chronic illnesses. Changes instituted later in life, after diseases are apparent, have little effect, and then only delay the progression of fatal complications. (p. 175)

Patient life-style is acquired via intra-family transmission of coping patterns in health and disease and may be in conflict with those of the physician and physician's recommendations. This ultimately may frustrate the prescribed medical regimen of the attending physician. Pellegrino (1973) has recognized that patient response to the stress of illness—pathology, acute and chronic—may be related less to immediate nurse-physician ministrations than to the values each places on life, the purpose of human existence, and all those beliefs constituting the image of ourselves and our world.

Pellegrino traces the influence of Hippocratic medicine and its "uneasy marriage" to Ionian natural philosophy and its continuing influence on the maturation of medical practice and philosophy. However, he seems to have overlooked the important influence of the early Judaic culture and the subsequent birth and development of Christian influence. Christianity as a way of life clearly has cultural roots in the Grecian era before Christ, but for obvious reasons Christianity through Jesus is more an outgrowth of the Judaic culture that preceded Christianity.

Clearly, if Grecian philosophy had prevailed, patient care, patient behavior, and the role of the aged in health and disease would now be substantially different. In the ancient world of the Greeks and Romans, old people were frequently put out of the way, especially in time of need. The aged were frequently left to die of hunger and exposure to wild beasts.

Judaic philosophy was in contrast to this practice and advocated a reverence for the aged: "Honor the hoary head in the face of an old man . . ." (Lev. 19:32); "Despise not your mother when she is old . . ." (Pro. 23:22); "With the aged there is wisdom and in length of days there is understanding" (Job 12:12), and "There is beauty of the face in ripe old age" (Eccles. 26:17). In the Jewish tradition, children were charged with the duty of providing for parents even when it involved the greatest of sacrifices, the necessity of begging for them.

Judaism thus condemns callousness for life in general and for the aged in particular and pronounces strong commitments for the healing of the sick. This support of the disadvantaged was of paramount significance in the Jewish way of life, even as the latter cultural philosophy was transmitted to the succeeding Christian era.

Christianity's commitment to uphold the sick, and Christ's particular concern for alleviating mental as well as physical afflictions, is repeatedly recorded in the Bible. In one translation the word "sick" appears 86 times and variants of health and healing appear no fewer than 158 times. The unity of the Jewish and Christian scriptures is nowhere more clearly expressed than when Jesus, beginning his ministry, quotes the words of Isaiah: "The Spirit of the Lord God is upon me . . . to bring good tidings to the afflicted, he has sent me to bind up the brokenhearted . . ." (Isaiah 61:1-2; Luke 4:18-19). Thus, the aged in our society, in illness and health, are in the possession of a substantial religious-cultural assurance that their place in society, when well or ill, can be fulfilled and their needs provided.

Patient-physician relationships are, however, confounded by changing tides of influence. Freidson, as reported by Branson (1973), declared,

> Medicine's position today is akin to that of the State religions yesterday. There is an officially approved monopoly of the right to define health and illness and to treat illness, and that the stigma of having been a deviant (ill) stays with the diseased person even after he has recovered. (p. 20)

Parsons (1958) identified illness as associated with sin, a social role, indicative of deviance, and thus physicians functioned as both physician and priest. As the priest-physician role diminishes in today's environment, increasing self-determination for patient and society threatens medicine's independence of action so traditional in our culture.

When the aged ill can utilize cultural safeguards and the physician is permitted to apply his art, skill, and science appropriately, disabilities of the aged can be cured; if not cured, ameliorated; and if not ameliorated, palliated.

Frequently, however, the aged ill may distort their inherent rights in demanding support, attention, comfort, and succor by virtue of rights inherent in the role of the sick. This may result in dependency, immobilization, chronic depression, and in physical, emotional, and social dysfunction in excess of an observable physical pathology or related disability. The provider of care, who is enjoined to meet the needs of the ill elderly, may then perceive the clinical experience as culminating in frustration, continued guilt, despair, professional exhaustion, and not infrequently, rising frustration and anger towards the disabled patient. Both patient and physician may thus be caught in a mutually self-destructive living process.

Case presentations of the ill, institutionalized aged may demonstrate this paradox of increasing disability in a social, medical, and nursing milieu, where providers of care, as well as the patient, fail in their expectations and perceptions of illness in the aged.

Case Number One

A seventy-eight year-old woman presents with mild to moderate, inactive rheumatoid arthritis with 10 to 15 percent loss in range of motion at the shoulder, hip, and knee joints. The patient has been essentially wheelchair-bound for seven years, although capable of ambulation. She had lived alone at home, non-ambulatory, and had been successful in inducing several neighbors to do her shopping, cooking, and housekeeping over an extended period.

This childless patient's arthritis began some years prior to the death of her husband, eight years ago. Following his death, a prolonged period of depression ensued, continuing to date. One year after her husband's death the patient fell and sustained a fracture of the right femoral shaft, and her physical disability has been cemented since, her capacity for ambulation notwithstanding. During periods of exacerbation or of depression and anxiety, mild to moderate signs of organic brain syndrome surface. The latter subsides virtually completely with remission of depression, as has occurred since admission to the nursing home. When her dependency needs are met, fear and depression subside substantially.

Her general appearance and conduct are that of a pleasant and attractive, but defenseless, depressed, and frightened old lady. Even in the presence of the overt evidences of weakness and despair, her use of these qualities to demand and control providers of care is most impressive. Her success in having a variety of neighbors, physicians, nurses, and other medical personnel provide for her daily needs has alleviated the need for an increased level of activities of daily living.

In essence, the patient's total disability is in substantial excess of the severity of the arthritis present. When aided to her feet by professional staff, the patient can indeed maintain body weight. She is capable of coordinated walking movements but denies her ability for independent locomotion, even when walking with the use of a walker. The patient's rejection of ambulation is volitional. It would appear that successful ambulation and increased ADL may severely threaten the current homeostatic mechanisms of the patient and the several providers of care. She apparently has a desire for continued physical immobilization and psychosocial dependency.

COMMENT. The patient has learned to utilize the "sick role" of the aged person in this Judeo-Christian culture to pursue dependency needs that in this instance are self-defeating. The patient's persistent depression, anxiety, panic, and self-determination to retain control over providers of care have resulted in prolonged physical immobilization. This is manifested in the threat of contractures, muscle atrophy, muscle weakness, inability to arise from a chair unaided, inability to ambulate, continuing depression, social isolation and withdrawal in a premature preparation for death, even as she protests her desire to live. Utilizing the sick role of our society, the patient has unwittingly increased her dependency needs and the degree of disability, preventing full realization of the potential of ADL. Further, the providers of care, being motivated by the Judeo-Christian ethic to help the ill and support the downtrodden, have unfortunately, in the pursuit of the cultural rewards of providing such help, also engaged in a distortion, indeed, a misuse of the cultural ethic. Supported by this, the patient's tyranny over staff facilitates continued dependency and physical and mental illness. If effect, the treatment team has yielded effective leadership for the "good" of the patient.

Case Number Two

This fifty-six year-old woman suffered an episode of encephalitis at twenty years of age with resultant advanced, disabling Parkinsonism. The patient had surgery that provided partial relief of the classical disabilities of Parkinsonism, severe rigidity, tremor, and contractures. The patient experienced some minimal benefit with L-dopa therapy.

The patient is able to sit in a chair with marked flexion contracture deformities of the head and neck, hips, knees, elbows, shoulders, hands, and fingers. Only intermittently is she able to arise from a chair unaided. During standing and ambulation she has the typical propulsive gait of Parkinsonism with marked deformities in posture and motion. She has fallen twice and sustained fractures of the right and left femora. Cognitive functions are intact. Her mood and affect are conditioned by intermittent depression, anxiety, and temper tantrums. Changing mood and affect, intact cognitive functions notwithstanding, markedly influence the level of somatic performance. During periods of exacerbation of depression and anxiety, the patient is unable to arise from a chair or engage in ambulation; speech becomes virtually inaudible, sialorrhea increases, and falling episodes are experienced.

This patient's illness and disability are clearly a human tragedy and heavily have affected intra-family relationships. The lives of her siblings became entwined in the defeated aspirations and the bleak prognosis for effective life for their ill sister. This basically intact family unit remained dedicated to providing the emotional, physical, and social needs of the patient volitionally and in response to her severe disability. The entire household revolved around the needs of the patient. Even as siblings married, reared children, and moved from the nuclear home, they return weekly and continue a social life with the patient. On holidays and vacations the patient continued to participate in the family lives of sisters and brother.

During the patient's tenure in the nursing home, the now mature married sisters and brother on several occasions planned vacations for their respective families without inclusion of the patient. During such periods the patient's physical and emotional performance on the nursing home premises deteriorated sharply. There were frequent episodes of crying, increasing physical disability including loss of ambulation, and frequent falls. The patient even became incontinent of urine. Disability escalated until family members returned. When siblings reincorporated her into the family dynamics, the patient's performance in ADL improved sharply; indeed, she invariably improved as she regained control and recaptured the family's attentive services. The patient erroneously perceived family behavior as abandonment, and even the family erroneously perceived their activities as abandonment of the patient. The patient was able to verbalize her complete awareness of the process. In fact, when confronted with such behavior, the patient would smile in recognition of it. In anticipation of deterioration of patient performance, the family would return, guilt-ridden, indicating that they indeed had enjoyed themselves, that they had remained well as their sister had become ill, and that they were the cause of their sister's illness and increased disability.

COMMENT.This patient often used her disability to maintain sibling relationships at a family level consistent with an immature, non-growing family. When siblings attempted to mature and meet the needs of their own respective families, the patient's performance deteriorated sufficiently to recapture her family's interest. Married siblings thus were inhibited from increasing growth potential of their own families. Thus, in a perverse use of the Judeo-Christian ethic with respect to illness, the patient periodically experienced self-induced increased disability in an attempt to retain influence over others. The professional providers of care were often ensnared in these shifting relationships. The ensnaring process accomplished by the patient's deterioration was reflected in increasing use of drugs in an effort to control increased evidence of Parkinsonism. Increased drug dosage on several occasions resulted in toxic effects. The prevailing sociocultural ethic in this instance was used by the patient, neither in her own nor in the family's best interest. Maladministration of drug therapy was an inadvertent associated experience.

Case Number Three

This seventy-three year-old man sustained a stroke with minimal to moderate aphasia. He was able to walk independently with cane and the typical hemiparetic gait. He was able to arise from a chair unaided; he required minimal aid in bathing and dressing and no assistance in feeding. He was able to communicate conversationally. The patient's behavior was characterized by chronic depression and marked anxiety. The latter often triggered unprovoked rage and threatening, hostile, combative episodes.

The patient's wife had died one year prior to the major stroke episode. Their marriage was described by the patient's daughter and only child as "stormy." The patient had been a successful marketing manager for a major furniture company.

The patient's daughter, married one year and in her late twenties, related that during her postpubescent period her father had made many overt sexual advances toward her. She was somewhat vague as to the actual incestuous behavior. She did admit to requiring formal psychiatric treatment in her late teens because of her ambivalent feelings toward the strong paternal figure and revulsion with the sexual experiences. She also admitted her parents' relationship was strained because of the father's attraction for her, and perhaps vice versa.

Following admission to the nursing home, the father had insisted on visits at least three times weekly from his daughter. When daughter and her husband were preoccupied either with their personal business affairs or vacation, on three separate occasions the patient's physical and emotional behavior deteriorated sharply. There was overt escalation of depression, lethargy, loss of comprehension and expressive speech, drooling, inability to feed himself, weight loss, incontinence of urine and stool, inability to arise from a chair unaided, and loss of safe ambulation. The level of the patient's activities of daily living deteriorated to a chair-bed level.

Deterioration in the patient's performance raised the clinical probabilities of recurrent stroke episodes, although no overt evidences of additional neuromuscular insults were noted. When the daughter resumed her regular visiting patterns, consistent with long-standing father-daughter relationships, the patient's level of behavioral and physical function improved considerably. The daughter's behavior, however, was one of ambivalence as she was caught between her increasing resentment for father, his demands upon her, and her need to meet his demands physically and emotionally. She was torn by guilt, anger, and love for father, and anxiety and guilt in a see-sawing fashion involving her relationship with her husband. When the patient's function deteriorated, the need for increased intensity of provider's services escalated and were delivered. In effect, the father's increasing disability, supported by the long-standing ethic of the Judeo-Christian society, resulted in the combined immobilization of patient, daughter, her husband, and treating staff.

COMMENT. It is patent that the waxing and waning of the patient's functional capacity was not dictated by increments of somatic disability or specific tissue pathology but was in fact related to attempts to reestablish familiar psychosocial pathology between father and daughter, her newer and more mature emotional and social abilities notwithstanding. The capacity of the patient to function in such fashion was supported by the acceptable dependency of the sickness symbol firmly embedded in the cultural ethic of illness. Thus, a perversion of the treatment process of the patient, the emotional maturation process of the daughter and her husband, and a distortion of the patient's clinical course and the treatment process of the providers of care occurred.

Case Number Four

An eighty-six year-old woman was admitted to the nursing home for continuing management of a chronic, recurrent venous ulceration of the left leg. Several years previously she had experienced a fall and sustained a fracture of the left hip with surgical reduction and fixation.

The patient was anxious and depressed and presented with minimal to moderate organic brain syndrome during exacerbations of emotional distress. She was a dependent, demanding, angry individual who preferred a wheelchair level of activities of daily living. On demand, however, she could arise from a chair unaided; she was able to bear body weight and engage in coordinated walking movements with the use of a cane. During locomotion, though, she insisted on aid with direct nurse contact. Without such contact she would threaten to fall; she would stand in her tracks and pitch to the right or left unless direct physical support was available. There was no obvious neurological pathology to account for dysfunction in ambulation. Essentially, the patient was a social isolate who, when brought into a community recreation area, would participate peripherally rather than engage in direct programs with patient peers. She was an observer rather than a participant. Thus, the patient clearly required a greater degree of nursing and medical management than anticipated on the basis of actual identifiable pathology and related dysfunction.

During her clinical course the patient was noted to suffer with progressive weight loss, losing almost twenty pounds. Initially she declared, "I have a poor appetite." Subsequently she claimed she was "vomiting every day." When nurses were requested to observe the vomiting process, the nurses were compelled to follow the patient into the bathroom area where the patient was noted to induce vomiting digitally.

The patient finally admitted she was in the process of a feud with her roommate. The basis for the conflict was not clearly delineated, except "I don't like her. I don't want to be here with her." When the patient was placed in another room the vomiting ceased, weight gain ensued, and ambulation improved to the preconflict level.

Additional history revealed the patient had been inducing vomiting since early childhood when she learned her father, whom she loved, had been found in process of extramarital sexual relationships. Thus, the patient was raised in a home split by dissatisfaction and insecurity. The patient's anger was directed towards father, mother, herself, and subsequently others during the course of her life. The patient's anger and anxiety was expressed with digitally induced vomiting.

The patient's only child, a son, related that his mother and father had a poor relationship. He described his mother as "A crabby, angry, disagreeable person" and that neither he nor his wife could live with her. "She's better off with you than in my home." His reluctant tolerance for his mother was obvious.

COMMENT. As a "sick person" the patient was entitled to care in this society, above and beyond that received by the well aged person. The patient utilized the self-induced illness to strike out at her roommate and manipulate a treating staff, initially, in her distorted interest. Paradoxically, her behavior caused revulsion against her by other patients (as she began to induce vomiting at the dining table), staff, and her son. All these intermingled events swirled in a not easily definable system of forces set loose by the patient during periods of clinging to maladaption to life events and misuse of an ethic system in behalf of self and the immediate interpersonal environment.

This case illustrates the system of interpersonal arrangements triggered by coping mechanisms of an aged patient in which the ethic of sickness in our society initially provides advantages to the sick, but when overutilized may result in increased immobilization of the patient, increased social isolation, a deteriorating course in the physical, emotional, and social aspects of daily living, and not the least, a conflicted interpersonal system where unsophisticated providers of services may be rendered ineffective.

Implications

In the case presentations above, chosen for their typicism rather than atypicism in the institutionalized ill aged, there is generally no relief of the patient's symptoms and no cure of disease as the patient pursues a course of life-style inimicable to improved quality of life and activities of daily living. Improved functioning is traded for control and domination of the external and interpersonal environment as a means of assuaging a personal sense of loss, deprivation, and anger. The positive use of the

Judeo-Christian ethic towards illness can be anticipated to culminate in either cure, amelioration, or palliation, whereas misuse or maladaptation of the same ethic is an ensnaring process that ultimately functions to the disadvantage of the sick and all those in attendance of the sick.

The ill aged in this instance superimpose a personal set of values upon societal general values with discordant results. The so-called "poorly motivated" patient, or the patient who functions in the pursuit of "secondary gains" of illness, does not function in a vacuum of a value system but as Clauser states (1976): "Without doubt we are all constantly being guided by moral considerations."

Clauser also claims, "We should not allow our conceptual struggle over the very difficult cases to hide the fact that moral deliberations give clear and unambiguous direction in most of our daily dealings." While patient, family, and provider of care in the above cases are in constant moral deliberation with each other and themselves, however, these deliberations provide neither a clear nor unambiguous signal to any of those so involved.

In a plea to make medicine more intelligible, Pellegrino (1973) espouses the pursuit of a philosophy of medicine in order to understand why we make certain decisions and what values underlie those decisions. He writes, "What theory of man energizes our clinical decisions? What epistemic bias and what logical pathway do we follow?" Additionally, Toulmin (1976) has noted:

> The patient's way of viewing the doctor, the profession and medical knowledge generally likewise shapes his expectations about the treatment, the understanding and the continuity of concern he will get from the doctor. If physician and patient have contrary ideas about the character and claims of medical knowledge, they are liable to end up with conflicting notions on the nature, terms and obligations of the professional relationship. (p.33)

There are few attempts to identify the basic principles of the cultural substrate in which patient-physician relationships are managed. Indeed, the basic principles of this Judeo-Christian culture appear to be a constantly evolving state. Clearly, the ethics and value systems of a society change, and in the evolution of such change it is imperative to identify the prevailing basic principles of the culture applicable to current clinical decision making. The term "culturally oriented" thus assumes a common understanding of a blurred and indistinct value system. Since patients, physicians, clergy, and other members of society generally harbor conflicted attitudes, it is understandable that providers of care are prone to distort the fundamental mission of our culture, to aid the sick, the downtrodden, the poor, and the deprived.

To prevent such distortion, the first step is an increased awareness of the distortion and the realization that healing involves more than the physical expression of illness. Underlying the secondary gains of illness is a sickness that comes closer to the domain of the physician-priest before the split in healing. Those nursing homes, extended care facilities, and other institutions committed to the total care of the ill aged will be concerned that the values of the Judeo-Christian tradition are not misused, but that the goal be to assist the aged affirm life in relationship with God, self, community and environment in a way that nurtures and celebrates wholeness. In those cases in which treatment is perhaps too late or the reasons for the secondary uses of illness too deeply rooted to be liberated, then, only after every attempt has failed, the physician and all called to minister must accept their own limitations without guilt or a sense of failure.

It is here that the medical profession and those who minister are in danger of disassociating themselves from the ill aged saying that nothing can be done. The religious community and those nursing homes and extended care facilities committed to the care of the whole person can bring to bear the very best of the Judeo-Christian tradition. Every effort should be made to assist the ill aged away from the misuse of sickness. Those who cannot be freed from their past, and consequently present dependencies, should of course receive the support necessary for their survival, but only after all attempts to free that patient from the misuse of dependency have failed.

The Judeo-Christian community can make a significant difference here. Grounded in Judaism is the love of God for a people who at times do not have any quality that is lovable (Hosea 2:23). In the Christian tradition it is the *agape* love of God—accepting that which is unacceptable, which is distinguished from *eros* or love primarily for the satisfaction and self-fulfillment received from another person. Heschell (1971) wrote: "The test of a people is how it behaves toward the old. It is easy to love children. Even tyrants and dictators make a point of being fond of children. But the affection and care of the old, the incurable, the helpless, are the true gold mines of a culture." (p.31)

The best of the Judeo-Christian tradition can make such gold mines a reality by understanding the misuse of its own commitment to care for the sick and ill aged while making every effort to free them and our culture from misuse of sickness. Where it cannot succeed, the ill aged can still find acceptance even if they cannot accept themselves.

REFERENCES

Branson, R. The secularizaiton of American medicine. *the Hastings Center Studies*, 1973, *1*, 17-21.

Clauser, K.D. Medical ethics, some uses and abuses and limitations. *The New England Journal of Medicine*, 1976, *293*, 385.

Ellis, J.R. Human values in medical education. *Annual Oration of the Society for Health and Human Values*, delivered Nov. 2, 1975, Washington, D.C.

Heschel, A.J. To grow in wisdom. *The Christian Ministry*, 1971, *2* (No. 2), 31-37.

Parsons, T. Definitions of health and illness in the light of American values and social structure. In E.G. Jaco (Ed.), *Patients, physicians, and illness*. New York: Free Press, 1958.

Pellegrino, E.D. Medicine and philosophy. *Annual Oration of the Society for Health and Human Values*, delivered Nov. 8, 1973, Washington, D.C.

Toulmin, S. The nature of physician's understanding. *Medicine and Philosophy*, 1976, *1*, 33.

Chapter 17

THE ROLE OF RELIGION IN THE MATURATION OF THE AUTONOMOUS OLDER ADULT

ANN VINSON

Doctor Maxwell Maltz, a plastic surgeon in New York City, made what he thought was a very meaningful discovery, and it was. He found that although he could make people look great on the outside, they often felt terrible within. He wondered why it was that he could repair the flesh but not restore the spirit. "It opened up a whole new horizon to me," he said. "I came to realize that the inner scars were far more disabling to people, but that they could remove them with a little compassion and respect for themselves." Acting on the divine principle of the value of each individual, he began helping people to become aware of the God-like quality in man. "It's a spiritual thing," he said. "It's not a new religion or a cult, but the active application of fundamental principles that sustain our sense of worth and dignity."

In exploring the role of religion in the development of an independent older adult, some concepts that are an integral part of the Judeo-Christian tradition should be examined. What is God? Does one's concept of God and His relationship to man and the universe affect the quality of life, its vitality, and its usefulness? Is the way we think about these things as much a determinant of life satisfaction as are material possessions and human companionship, important as these may be?

Much of what we are is the result of the way we think. Age is a mental concept. The late Jack Benny said, "Age is a matter of mind. If you don't mind, it doesn't matter." The Bible records lucid examples of persons who were brought into pitiful plights because of doleful thinking. By changing their thought, each was enabled to see that despondency and futility are not the natural state of man. The patriarch Job, because of reversals in his human affairs, longed for death. He lamented, "Wherefore is light given to him that is in misery, and life to the bitter in soul; which long for death but it commeth not; and dig for it more than hidden treasure; which rejoice exceedingly, and are glad when they can find the grave" (Job 3:20-22). One of Job's friends challenged the negativism. "Thou shalt forget thy misery, and remember it as waters that pass away," he said. "And thine age shall be clearer than the noonday; thou shalt shine forth, thou shalt be as the morning" (Job 11:16,17). Job turned from self-pity and despair and began to seek a better understanding of God. When his idea of God changed, he could jubilantly exclaim, "I have heard of thee by the hearing of the ear; but now mine eye seeth thee." (Job 42:5).

This kind of seeing has nothing to do with the physical eye. It is the illumination that follows the willingness to give up preconceived notions and to accept new ideas. It means more than rearranging cherished beliefs. It begins by seeing that linking the two words "growing old" is not only incongruous but fallacious as well. Does growing necessarily entail getting old? Is there more than one way to grow? We can grow morose, disgruntled, or stolid. We can grow compassionate, happy, and wise. We can grow creatively, intellectually, spiritually. There is no age limit or termination point to the kind of growth that results from spiritual thinking.

Since World War II, and especially in the last two decades, the study of aging has become an "in" thing. There are many reasons for this: cultural, industrial, demographic. One thing is certain. There are many theories about aging: genetic, physiological, psychological, sociological. They all have one thing in common. Only the temporal nature of man is considered. For the most part, the spiritual nature of man is neglected. This is not difficult to understand. The tools of research have been borrowed from models suitable for the study of nature but not for the study of the whole man.

Sacher (1965) finds it startling that psychologists and gerontologists accept the same view about aging as the geneticists. These social disciplines infer that biochemists will make the discoveries and that others will be satisfied to describe what geneticists have found. This is a dubious approach to the study of aging. The physical aspect of man sheds little light on the man who is made in the image and likeness of God. There are no valid instruments for measuring and evaluating the spiritual qualities of love, joy, wholeness, wisdom, or integrity.

One of the most precious increments that accrues with the years is a source of satisfaction if one has developed the mental acumen and spiritual resource to recognize this. Whether one simply grows old or develops into a mature creative person is more a matter of choice than most individuals are willing to admit. The children of Israel learned this from Moses, who spiritually instructed them in the choices they had: "I call heaven and earth to record this day against you, that I have set before you life and death, blessing and cursing; therefore choose life, that both thou and thy seed shall live" (Deut. 30:19).

Growth and development go on continually; discontinuities, challenges, and crises, if viewed correctly, can aid in the maturation of an autonomous older person. Erikson (1963) has contributed valuable concepts to the understanding of human development. By studying the psychosocial histories of certain individuals, he traces development through the human life cycle. His life cycle theory consists of eight stages, each of which describes a psychosocial event that takes place as man develops. Such an event requires for its resolution an interplay of qualities, one more favorable than the other. From this interplay should develop a new quality that provides the individual with strength to progress. Very briefly, Erikson's theory is this: In the first stage, the infant tests the qualities of trust and distrust in the parental relationship. If a sense of trust develops, hope arises. The second stage tests autonomy and shame. If a child is permitted freedom to explore his environment, there develops the will to progress.

The third stage tests initiative and guilt. If the child is encouraged and given opportunity to try his skills, there emerges from this stage purpose. The fourth stage tests industry and inferiority from which emerges competence or its opposite. The fifth stage tests identity and identity confusion, in which fidelity should emerge as one associates with his peers. Intimacy and isolation are tested in young adulthood and from this sixth stage emerges love or its opposite. The seventh stage tests generativity and self-absorption. This stage generally occurs in middle age when one is either concerned with others or becomes inordinately concerned with self. From this stage emerges care. The eighth stage tests integrity versus despair. When viewed on a continuum, this stage has broad implications for gerontology. It suggests that the emergence of wisdom or its opposite (disgust and despair) can adversely or favorably affect individual behavior and attitudes in the later years. It also suggests that the acceptance or rejection of self is a highly differential process shaped in part by the quality of a personal and cultural milieu that anteceded the present stage.

The question that arises from a careful perusal of Erikson's life cycle theory is whether the positive qualities that may emerge at each stage are human or divine attributes. If one believes that faith, hope, love, and wisdom are human qualities, they then become subject to change and conflicting interpretation. If, however, they are thought to be divine qualities, they reflect the nature of God and are immutable.

These two dichotomous positions have led us to postulate a ninth stage in human development that need not be sequential but might be thought of as a part of prior stages. This ninth stage tests spirituality versus materiality, from which there may emerge spiritual understanding. By exercising spiritual faculties and perception, a higher concept of God is obtained.

Some of my research has involved observing and interviewing two groups of older adults, one urban, one rural. The quality of their spiritual understanding was found to have a direct impact not only on life satisfaction but on the ability of the individual to meet challenges and to surmount difficulties. One instance from this research will suffice. A couple (he 94; she 96) lived on a farm and raised cucumbers that they sold to a local cannery. The wife had picked cucumbers the day I visited; she had also baked bread, which was on the kitchen table. Free of anxiety and fear, they talked of their life together. "Each morning," the wife said, "I go to the window and thank God for another day."

Day always dawns to those who are spiritually awake. To those who believe that life is eternal, the darkness called death is neither an event nor a reality. The subject of death is very much a part of gerontological literature. While researchers dissect, analyze, and compartmentalize death into stages, older adults with whom I visited, and who have glimpsed something of immortality, have already figuratively walked through the valley of the shadow and have no intention of staying there. The independence of thought that has helped develop them into mature individuals made them certain there were other worlds to explore.

The fear of death needs to be eradicated, and it can be when it becomes more generally understood that physicality is not the whole of man or a part of man's essential nature. Physical scientists no longer consider the actuality of matter but have advanced into the field of energy and beyond. An individual who leaves a material body behind might be compared to a jet that is lost in the distance but whose vapor stream indicates that there is a force out front, although no discernible object can be seen with the naked eye.

Birth and death are relative terms. An island is born, a battery goes dead. The Elizabethan poet John Donne wrote:

> Death be not proud, though some have called thee Mighty and dreadful,
> for thou are not soe, For those whom thou thinkest, thou dost overthrow,
> Die not, poore death, nor yet canst thou kill me.
>
> (1967, p.342)

In no other area does one have such complete freedom to accept or reject a concept than in the realm of thought. Our basic values, the moral and spiritual principles we live by, are frequently predicated on what we have been taught or on how we have reinterpreted what we have learned. On our choices hinge much of our growth and development. Sir Thomas More said, "A man is nothing, but what he believes and acts upon." The choices one makes have a direct bearing on maturation, autonomy, and maturity. The later years provide so many kinds of freedom, not the least of which is mental freedom. Another kind of freedom, which to many may seem demeaning, comes with the lessening of career and family responsibilities. Viewed correctly, this release from social and family pressures can provide unexcelled opportunities for finding one's self and being one's self. It is a time to be free from remorse, to forgive one's self by knowing that there is nothing more corrosive and enfeebling than regret. Jesus explained how this could be done, "Ye shall know the truth, and the truth shall make you free." (John 8:32).

The Bible contains many truths that can be understood through the quality of spiritual understanding, which evolves in the ninth stage of development that we have postulated. For instance, those things that are considered basic needs and too often lacking in the later years are discussed in the Bible. As an illustration, the need for food, clothing, and shelter was not ignored by Jesus. He reminded his hearers to consider the lilies of the field and the birds of the air and concluded by saying, "Therefore take no thought, saying, what shall we eat? or What shall we drink? or, Wherewithal shall we be clothed? Your heavenly Father knoweth that ye have need of all these things. But seek ye first the kingdom of God, and his righteousness; and all these things shall be added unto you." (Mat. 6:31-33).

Neogenic neurosis, that emptiness that pervades too many stages of life but more particularly the later years, can be eradicated by cultivating spiritual well-being. Benjamin Franklin once spoke of the smallest, insignificant bundle in the world as being "a man wrapped up in himself." The central core of Christianity is selflessness, not self-centeredness. Religion is not a form of therapy that turns one inward. The later years provide unparalleled ways in which one can share the wisdom, skills, and insightful understanding acquired only by the experience called living. An eighty-four-year-old woman we know was taking care of her fifty-year-old daughter who had returned home mentally and physically broken. Dismissing condescension she explained, "I have always believed that one should justify his existence." One who was constantly occupied doing necessary tasks for her peers in the community said, "When you cast your bread upon the water, it comes back cake."

The later years can be filled with creativity, and they also provide the extra bonus of being alone when one chooses. There is so much about aging we have not thought out. Until spiritual well-being becomes the rule and not the exception, aging will continue to be an artifact of our philosophical environment, a concept formed artificially by an industrial society, medical and genetic theories, and social and psychological experimentation. The later years may not be easy but we can make them worthwhile. If the going gets rough at times, borrow the technique of a small boy who with his father was caught in the middle of the street during rush hour. The father looked at the frightened face and asked, "Shall I take your hand?" "No," said the boy, "I would like to take yours."

REFERENCES

Donne, John. *The complete poetry of John Donne.* New York: Doubleday, 1967.
Erikson, Erik. *Childhood and society.* New York: Norton, 1963.
Sacher, George A. *Psychobiology of aging.* New York: Springer, 1965.

Section IV
SPIRITUAL WELL-BEING IN RELATION TO THE COMMUNITY

Chapter 18

SPIRITUAL WELL-BEING OF THE ELDERLY IN RELATION TO THE COMMUNITY

MOTHER M. BERNADETTE DE LOURDES

Broadly, community can be defined as a place where persons live out various activities of life. It is a place where people are born, where they grow, where they work, where they meet and socialize, and where they love and marry. It is a place where a person may associate with every endeavor of life. It is a true statement that no man can live alone, no man is an island. When men and women associate, they develop a relationship that is known as community. The accepted etymological derivation of the word community is from the Latin *cum*, meaning with, and *munificus*, giving a gift. Following the idea suggested by this derivation, we evolve the meaning of community; it is a place and situation in which human beings share gifts. One way that we might perceive gifts would be to place them into four categories: physical, psychological, social, and spiritual. The primary evidence of the existence of a real community, whether it is a large city or a tiny village, is a sharing of spiritual gifts in the religious context.

The aging should not be separated from other age groups in the process of seeking spiritual well-being. In recognizing free and independent partnerships in every spiritual assembly, older adults should be accepted as equals. Just as special provision is made, however, in every spiritual assembly for other age groups, such as children and teenagers, special consideration could give increased opportunity to the elderly to express and fulfill their particular needs and desires. Thought should be given to such conveniences, as a practical matter, as ramps instead of steps so that older persons with physical limitations may be able to enter places of worship. Many older people find it difficult to sit for a long period of time in uncomfortable seats. Some older people have hearing impairments and need increased volume in order to hear what is being said. Good lighting is important for the elderly.

In every community, the spiritual relationship mandates the need to increase and bring to perfection the affirmation that every aging person has the resources available for a full spiritual life. Our best promise is in continuing the effort to hold to and advance the resources in each community that give the aging an opportunity to live in an atmosphere of spiritual well-being. On this topic, we know that some of the oldest wisdom of mankind concerning relationships with the aging can be found in the Bible.

These biblical teachings constitute the Judeo-Christian philosophy of care, concern, and compassion. The supreme worth of every human being, created to the image and likeness of God, is one of the basic teachings of the Bible. Studies have indicated that belief in God reaches its highest levels and is of the greatest intensity in the later years of life. In Ecclesiastes we read, "Despise not a man in old age, for we also shall become old." Proverbs tells us, "Old age is a kind of dignity when it is found in the ways of justice." Spiritual well-being makes the older person secure because it assures him that this life is not the end but merely a preparation for the next.

It has been said that we are our brother's keeper. No matter how busy we are, we should try to find time to be concerned about the aging who need our assistance in a wide variety of ways. The parable of the good Samaritan can be seen as an excellent example. He too was busy. He was on a mission but he saw a man in need. He had a true awareness of the needs of his fellowman. He had compassion. He had feeling for the injured man. He went to him and showed his concern and willingness to offer help. He provided aid, transportation, shelter, financial assistance, and genuine concern. Further, he promised to come back to check on the well-being of the injured man.

The aging need to be accepted and reassured. It has been said that we prove the extent of our love for God by the love we bestow on our neighbors, and everyone is our neighbor. Spiritual well-being is a vital part of man's life throughout the years, but it becomes more vital toward the end of life. When the older person finds that his productive years are seemingly past and that he must look forward to a future of limited activities, religion offers him the stimulus to use to the maximum the talents and abilities that are still his. Religion proves and convinces the older person that he is most precious in the eyes of his Creator, that his soul is unique and has a special place in God's plan. It has been said that the test of a society is how it behaves towards its elderly, remembering with gratitude the contributions that they have made throughout their lives.

The delegates to the Section on Spiritual Well-Being of 1971 White House Conference on Aging concluded that to ignore or attempt to separate the need to fulfill the spiritual well-being of a man from attempts to satisfy his physical, material, and social needs is to fail to understand the meaning of God and the meaning of man. Whether it is the concern for education, employment, health, housing, income, nutrition, retirement, or transportation, the proper solution involves personal identification, social acceptance, and human dignity. We cannot separate the body from the soul.

It would be possible to make a long list of the spiritual and material needs of the aging; we will mention just a few. First is the older person's relationship with God and other people. Second, the right of choice to make his or her own decisions should not be taken away unless the person is completely incompetent. Third is that we must recognize each older person as an individual who is unique, realizing that we are not members of a homogeneous group. Fourth is to be treated as a person deserving of love, respect, and compassion. Fifth is to recognize that the last period of life is part of the life cycle, a time of preparation for the future life. It should be an exciting period, not a dismal or dreary period of life. Finally, loneliness can be a real cause of suffering to older persons, especially to those who have severe physical or mental limitations. It will particularly affect those whose closest family members or friends have preceded them by death. The practice of prayer can be very important to the isolated person. In prayer one can sense the presence of God that dispells loneliness.

Synagogues and churches must have an awareness and a

concern not only for the spiritual needs of the aging but also for their physical, emotional, environmental, and social needs. The body and the soul are very closely united and related. Today's population of older persons is entitled to the very best in quality of care and the ready availability of all the services and programs needed to meet their needs. Hopefully, through the partnership of programs under governmental and religious auspices, a wide variety of services can be initiated and developed in local communities.

Since the needs of the aging are many and varied, let us mention just a few services that could be provided for in our communities. Heading the list are services that enable the older person to continue to live in his or her own home. This is not simply a matter of economics. A person can be very well off financially, but if the services are not available, he is still deprived. We need different kinds of health care delivery systems, and facilities providing many services in various aspects of health care. We need day care centers for older adults who are not capable of staying home alone during the day, and we need outreach to locate these people. These programs can and are many times related to synagogues and churches. We need information and referral services. Some older people have no idea where to go to get information they need. Certainly we need social services; older people need legal services, assistance with financial matters, and other kinds of services too numerous to mention. They need preparation for retirement. They need educational programs and services.

Recognizing the varied and changing needs of the older person, it would seem that it would be highly desirable to have a center, a social services center, where these services could be provided. Such a total program would be a valuable resource to the community. It would seem that synagogues and churches, with the assistance of federal, state, and local government and other public agencies, could stimulate and develop such resource centers. This would be a community-based program and would enhance the spiritual well-being of the aging and other members of the community.

In conclusion, spiritual well-being and religion play an

important part in the lives of persons of all ages. Older citizens, however, derive special comfort and consolation from religion and in turn it furnishes many outlets for useful and prayerful activities that nourish not only the spirit but the mind and body as well. All faiths acknowledge a supreme, sovereign Creator who is a law giver, a judge, and the one who gives a final reward. We are united in our firm conviction that God must play an all-important part in the life of each one of us. We believe that He created us, that He cares for us, and that He loves us singularly and together with the love He has proven in countless ways. We affirm that spiritual well-being supercedes all other values. We declare that spiritual well-being is a supreme affirmation of life.

STRANGERS AND PILGRIMS
ON THE EARTH

STANLEY V. MICHAEL

Some religious groups claim that evangelical Christians es-
pouse a "pie-in-the-sky" theology that makes them "so
heavenly minded they are of no earthly good." Within the
evangelical tradition there is a conservative position that borders
on what many people still refer to as fundamentalism. Of this
group William Hordern (1968) observed, "The heart of fundamentalism is in its concern for salvation. The only really
important question is, 'Have you been saved?'" (p. 60).

As evangelical Christians, we do not apologize for the salvation
emphasis of our religious tradition. We believe that an individual
relationship with God will reach its ultimateness only in the life
to come. Indeed, we *do* believe that the most important question
the church, any church, can ask and should be asking, today or
any day, is "Have you been saved?"

Any true understanding of being saved is that life does extend
beyond our pilgrimage here to an eternal relationship with God.
This philosophy is grounded in Scripture passages such as
Hebrews 13:14: "For here we do not have an enduring city, but we
are looking for the city that is to come." This is translated into an
understanding of the church's responsibilities to society as well as
into a theology of aging.

Taken to an extreme, a concern for adequately preparing for an
afterlife can minimize the vast array of very real and important
needs each individual faces in this temporal existence. In reaction
to those who sought to establish the kingdom of God on earth
only through the education and reformation of mankind, early
fundamentalists shunned anything that might be considered
what they disparagingly referred to as the "social gospel." This
overreaction on the part of some conservative Christians created

142

a tendency to emphasize the spiritual needs of man to the near exclusion of physical, social, emotional, and material considerations.

In more recent years, evangelicals in general have taken greater measures to attach more importance to the truth presented in the Epistle of James:

> What good is it, my brothers, if a man claims to have faith in God but has no deeds? Can such faith save him? Suppose a brother or sister is without clothes and daily food. If one of you says to him, 'Go, I wish you well; keep warm and well fed,' but does nothing about his physical needs, what good is it? In the same way, faith by itself, if it is not accompanied by action, is dead. (2:14-17)

A decade ago, Sherwood Eliot Wirt (1967) observed a growing trend in evangelical thinking. He said that the typical gospel church of today still wants its minister to be fervent, dedicated, evangelistic, and biblically oriented, but today's congregation also requires a dimension that was much less important in past years. The evangelical minister must be in tune with the social ferment about him, aware of the truth that God is in the world as well as in the church. Some evangelical seminaries are taking the lead in this area: "Without forsaking the spiritual heritage of the faith, without reducing the content of the Bible, they are implanting in their men and women students the conviction that the Christian, because he is a member of the human race, has inescapable responsibilities to society" (Wirt, 1967, p.3).

A by-product of an awareness of the Christian's place in the human race has been an increased interest in the phenomenon of aging. For many years, even the most conservative Christian groups have recognized a responsibility to provide care, by way of nursing homes for example, to the small minority of senior adults who have physical or mental handicaps that prevent a viably independent place in society at large.

In the Assemblies of God, there is functioning a permanent committee on aging. Areas of consideration include coordinating services, materials, films, and other ministries on behalf of senior citizens. In the early 1930s a program began which gave financial assistance to the denomination's aged ministers and widows who did not have adequate retirement resources. A retirement facility was established especially for retired ministers and missionaries. This has now expanded to a complete retirement village.

An increasing number of Assembly of God churches have on their staff a senior adult minister whose chief ministry is to the aged. These ministers contribute to the spiritual well-being of many who are not able to attend regular worship services. Programs of regular visitation keep alive the contact needed for a feeling of mutual need. For many years large print Sunday School materials have been provided. The blind elderly have also been helped through a religious Braille program and tape library.

This concern for the aged has also been broadened to a cognizance that residents of nursing homes are but a small percentage of older men and women among us and, further, that this significant group is made up of individuals with unique needs and worth. We have been recognizing that it is not enough to continue nurturing relationships with God, however important that might be. The church must be concerned about the total person, all aspects of an individual's well-being, taking into particular consideration a person's interaction with the multi-faceted process of aging. Attention must be given to each individual's relationships to self, community, and environment.

Important considerations in ministry to senior adults must include building and maintaining a healthy self-image, encouraging a climate that will make possible a mutually beneficial reciprocity between the individual and the community as a whole, and guaranteeing a reasonable degree of physical comfort through responsible and compassionate use of available resources.

We are excited about this potential of Christian service that evangelicals are showing in aging and the aged and in providing an important ministry to the total person, but the temporal needs of the aged must be kept in proper perspective. The first priority of the church always must be in building a relationship with God, for this alone is eternal. As Jesus himself said, "What good is it for a man to gain the whole world, yet forfeit his soul?" (Mark 8:36).

The verse from Hebrews quoted earlier has been taken out of

context and pushed to extremes of irresponsibility. However, we still believe that in it lies an essential foundation for a concept of aging: For here we do not have an enduring city, but we are looking for the city that is to come.

What are the ramifications of this principle in the formulation of attitudes toward aging as it is applied to everyday situations in life? Does it mean that we constantly affirm our relationship to God and totally negate all apparent needs that grow out of our temporary residence on earth? This is not the case; rather, by looking at themselves as citizens of the city that is to come, those who thus live by faith in God are able to put aging into a proper perspective and have an adequate framework within which to formulate their responses to all aspects of life.

Aging as a Process

First, the "foreigner" on this earth recognizes that aging is one part of the total life process: "We are *looking* for the city that is to come." The age of sixty-five, or any other arbitrary number, does not signal the start of a final stage, the beginning of the end. Instead the person of faith can look forward to a continual movement of "becoming," of being "in process" as long as he lives.

Paul Pruyser (1975), in discussing the losses and gains of aging, observed: "The life course is neither upward or downward, but a forward movement full of new discoveries" (p. 102). This forward movement can and should occur until a person's last breath. Florida Scott-Maxwell (1968) expressed surprise at this discovery: "Age puzzles me. I thought it was a quiet time. My seventies were interesting, and fairly serene, but my eighties are passionate. I grow more intense as I age. To my own surprise I burst out with hot conviction" (p. 13).

To the individual who looks for the city that is to come, death is not to be feared or dreaded but anticipated as another step in the process of finding that eternal home.

Self-acceptance

The loss of self-acceptance is one of the most tragic problems the aged face. Recently a sixty-three-year-old man talked with a hospital chaplain shortly after learning he had acute leukemia: "I never expected to live as long as Methuselah, but I guess no matter how long you live, your life is still too short. What I really feel bad about is that there are some things I wish I had done differently. I just don't understand why I did some things." This man, like many others who approach the end of their lives, began to doubt his self-worth and wished he could live parts of his life over again.

Henri Nouwen and Walter Gaffney (1974) have observed that self-rejection can be an inner ostracism by which the aged may feel stripped of a feeling of self-worth and no longer be at home in their innermost life. With this sense of self-rejection often comes a fear of rejection by God. Even the Psalmist David expressed this concern: "Do not cast me off when old age comes, nor forsake me when my strength fails" (Psalm 71:9).

The person of faith has the reassurance from God's Word that he is, indeed, a person of intrinsic worth. The creation account in Genesis assures that man is made in the image of God. There is sanctity and worth in all life. In addition, both the Old and New Testaments demand special respect for those of old age, as well as affirming that length of days is a gift from God to be treasured dearly. In I Corinthians, the apostle Paul reminded each believer that he is an essential part of the body of Christ and thus worthy of honor. Of utmost importance is the fact that the believer can accept himself because God has accepted him through the work of His son: "And so Jesus suffered outside the city gate to make his people holy through his own blood" (Hebrews 13:12). The elderly sojourner can know he is accepted for who he is, not for what he has done.

This truth is especially significant in view of our competitive production-oriented society. Nouwen and Gaffney (1974) described the situation the elderly face: "The fear of becoming old in our Western world is, for the most part, determined by the fear of not being able to live up to the expectations of an environment in which you are what you can produce, achieve, have, and keep" (p. 26). The one whose citizenship is in heaven, in that city which is to come, can accept himself even when he might no longer meet society's demands of productivity. Because of God's acceptance through the suffering of Christ, the individual is free not to "do" but to "be."

Benefits of Community

As a member of the household of God, the elderly person on the earth has the right to expect certain benefits as a member of the family. In turn, the older members of the community have a responsibility to share their gifts with their fellow sojourners. As previously mentioned, the primary source of self-esteem for a person of faith is not found in what the person does but in his relationship with God through the completed work of Jesus. However, this does not negate the sense of satisfaction derived from contributing to other members of the community. In fact, almost immediately after focusing on the city that is to come, the writer of the Hebrew epistle exhorted believers: "And do not forget to do good and to share with others, for with such sacrifices God is pleased" (Hebrews 13:16).

Even though the fact often is overlooked, elder members of a community bring with them a body of knowledge and experience that younger members have not yet had an opportunity to obtain. Simone de Beauvoir (1972) relates a Balinese legend about the consequence of the custom of sacrificing and eating their old men. When there was not a single old man left and the traditions were lost, the young men realized that, literally, "no one could tell the top from the bottom."

Those who have traveled this way before can share some of their insights on the best way to get from here to there. The Song of Moses emphasized the importance of passing down lessons learned from past experience: "Remember the days of old, think of the generations long ago; ask your father to recount it and your elders to tell you the tale" (Deuteronomy 32:7).

In a similar manner, Solomon warned, "My son, observe your father's commands and do not reject the teaching of your mother;

wear them always next to your heart and bind them close about
your neck" (Proverbs 6:20).

Perhaps one of the most important contributions the old can
make to the young is simply by their presence making the young
aware of the entire life process, including aging and death. It is a
common tragedy that people avoid a confrontation with death
and thus avoid a reminder of their finiteness. Therefore, even in
death the elderly can contribute to the young.

The Pauline analogy of the Christian community as a body
points out the interdependence of the members of God's family.
Not only do the elderly contribute to the young, but the inverse is
also true. Though the person of faith thinks of himself as a
stranger and foreigner on earth, he still has very real needs now.
For example, the Harris poll commissioned by the National
Council on the Aging (1975) demonstrated that there are very
serious problems attributed to old age. The most commonly
mentioned problems associated with being old were poor health,
loneliness, financial problems, lack of independence, being
neglected or unwanted, and boredom. Obviously, not all old
people experience the same problems; each person has his own
unique set of needs. No one person is able to meet all the needs of
all the others in any given community. However, through a
responsible and compassionate use of available resources by all
members, the community of believers can guarantee a reasonable
degree of physical comfort and safety, intellectual stimulation,
and social interaction for fellow sojourners, including the aged.

When Things Look Dark

Even when the entire community works together for the
welfare of the aged, though, there will be some problems that
create hardships on individuals. Some common misfortunes that
often cannot be avoided are illness, accidents, loss of independence, and loss of loved ones. The concept of being a stranger on
the earth provides a vehicle for dealing with these and other
hardships. For the person of faith, hope can continue through all
circumstances.

Nouwen and Gaffney (1974) discuss the conversion from wishes to hope, which may be facilitated by the process of suffering. They speak of hope as being open-ended, built on the trust that promises will be fulfilled. The person of faith, by his very nature, is undergirded by this kind of trust in a God who will keep His promises, a God who has promised that He has prepared a place for His child in His house. It is in the adverse situations of life that the stranger and foreigner can find meaning in these words: "For we do not have an enduring city, but we are looking for the city that is to come. Through Jesus, therefore, let us continually offer to God a sacrifice of praise—the fruit of lips that confess his name" (Hebrews 13: 14-15).

The concept that the person who lives by faith is a foreigner and stranger on the earth has radical implications for our attitudes toward aging and our responsibilities toward the aged. For those who would take this idea seriously, there can be no excuse for ignoring or refusing to deal with the situations each aging person confronts in his life on earth.

REFERENCES

deBeauvoir, S. *The coming of age.* New York: C.P. Putnam's Sons, 1972.

Harris, L. & Associates. *The myth and reality of aging in America.* Washington, D.C.: National Council on the Aging, Inc., 1975.

Hordern, W. *A layman's guide to Protestant theology.* London: The Macmillan Company, Collier-Macmillan Ltd., 1968.

Nouwen, H.J.M. & Gaffney, W.J. *Aging.* Garden City, New York: Doubleday & Company, Inc., 1974.

Pruyser, P.W. Aging: Downward, upward, or forward? *Pastoral Psychology,* Winter 1975, *24,* 102-118.

Scott-Maxwell, F. *The measure of my days.* New York: Alfred A. Knopf, 1968.

Wirt, S.E. *The social conscience of the Evangelical.* New York: Harper & Row, Publishers, 1968.

Chapter 20

A HOLISTIC APPROACH
TO SPIRITUAL WELL-BEING*
ROBERT W. MCCLELLAN

"What shall we do?" is the spoken or silent question in the minds and hearts of many persons in the Judeo-Christian community when faced with the issue of ministry and older people. Behind the question often lurks guilt, apathy, fear, frustration, and perhaps even quiet despair. Clear answers have not been coming, some believe that hope is on the way.

Much significant work among older persons, on a large scale, has been done and is now being done across the country through multipurpose senior centers. The first known center for older people came into being in 1944 in New York City. The term "center" may mean whatever any person or group wishes it to mean. However, a general consensus as outlined by Maxwell (1962) is that a "center" is a designated place in which older people meet at least two days each week, under the guidance of paid leaders performing professional tasks. The multipurpose center focuses on basic needs such as food, shelter, clothing, health care, transportation, recreation, companionship and love, and a purpose for living. The *Directory of Senior Centers and Clubs: A National Resource* listed approximately 4,900 centers nationally and other important data on programs for older adults (Leanse and Wagner, 1974).

The community-accepted definition of "center" need not dissuade the religious community. There is no reason to limit the

---

*Some of the material in this chapter appeared in different form in Dr. McClellan's recent book, *Claiming a Frontier: Ministry and Older People.* Los Angeles: University of Southern California Press. Copyright © 1977, The Ethel Percy Andrus Gerontology Center. Used by permission of the author and the Ethel Percy Andrus Gerontolgy Center, University of Southern California, Los Angeles.

use of the word "center" in regard to churches and synagogues. One promising option for religious institutions is to create "centers" using their own local creativity and resources. What is essential is a well-conceived and well-conducted program that is broad enough to meet many of the needs of older persons; also essential is the older persons' involvement in the planning and conducting of the center's life.

The value of a center lies in its advantages for older persons, which are in addition to intergenerational experiences in family, congregational, or community groups. Advantages include a planned spectrum of programs to meet broad-scoped interests; continued input on a regular basis; and physical, mental, emotional, and spiritual stimulation through exposure, sharing, and learning. On the other hand, we must recognize open prejudice to centers due to ignorance of their purpose and program. Many persons hold stereotyped convictions that such places are for ghettoizing the feeble in mind and body. There may be a general resistance to identification with aging among the aged, thus causing reluctance of many older persons to become involved and stimulated.

An informal study by this author in 1974 revealed that while many congregations do "something" concerning older persons, most church-related programs for the elderly deal with bits and pieces. Few seem to have caught the holistic sense of need and opportunity and have programs that represent vision and concern.

Due to several factors, programs in the secular section have developed more rapidly and effectively than those in the religious sector. Some of the reasons for this include the recognition by specialists in gerontology of the needs of older people as revealed through research, funds made available through taxation and administered by governmental agencies, and program development and evaluation made possible by funds committed for this special purpose and carried on by trained professionals whose careers are dedicated to this field. The church and synagogue have largely proceeded on another course, including such factors as a lack of awareness of the needs of older persons, failure to consider older persons as a priority concern, limited funds to cover a ministry for all ages, and lack of trained leadership. We also lack a true theology of aging as well as denominationally sponsored materials and training opportunities.

Chatsworth Adult Center

The beginning of the Chatsworth Adult Center coincided with the beginning of interest in programs for older persons in the Point Loma Community Presbyterian Church, San Diego, California. An Older Adults Committee composed of seven members of the church was chosen and held its first meeting in January of 1974. The Committee included three older couples and one young woman with some academic background in gerontology.

The Committee reviewed the church rolls and found that more than 400 persons were over sixty years of age out of a total membership of approximately 2,000. Another 400 were estimated to be between fifty and sixty years old. It was concluded that little was being done in the church and community, except for pastoral care being given by members of the church staff. A list of possible needs was made through sharing of experiences, including such concerns as survival, safety, social, self-esteem, and spiritual necessities. The Committee determined to work toward developing a program for older members of the church and community that could lead to meeting some of the identified needs. The stance was one of openness and learning.

The first meeting of an unnamed group of older persons was held the following April. Approximately 40 (10%) older members of the church attended. Interest was genuine and the desire to continue was strong enough to encourage the Committee to pursue further exploration and activity. The larger group decided to begin to meet monthly and to expand the Older Adults Committee, thereafter called the Steering Committee, to a total of fourteen persons. The new group continued to meet weekly and began to seek the guidance of the Department on Aging, Catholic Community Services, Diocese of San Diego, and Senior Adult Services, San Diego. The group became aware of the Senior Centers in San Diego jointly sponsored by the Adult Education

Department of San Diego Community Colleges and Catholic Community Services.

The group of older people was ready by this time to consider moving from a local church expression of concern for meeting needs of older persons to a wider usefulness that might be accomplished through becoming one of the Senior Centers sponsored by the Adult Education Department of San Diego Community College and Catholic Community Services. After careful discussion the decision was made, and during October of 1974 it became the sixth in a series of such centers in metropolitan San Diego. The new arrangement provided for a paid Coordinator, responsible both to the Community Colleges and Catholic Community Services. This arrangement has worked to benefit the Center. Since that date weekly meetings have been held on Tuesdays from 9:00 am to 3:00 pm. The name Chatsworth Senior Center, chosen by the group at its initial meeting, was later changed by them to Chatsworth Adult Center. It was felt that the program and opportunity for growth would appeal to all adults. The significance of the name Chatsworth is that the church is located on Chatsworth Boulevard. The center has become a place for any and all who wish to attend, and thus is a genuine community and ecumenical resource.

Twelve Rejuvenating Techniques

Twelve Rejuvenating Techniques identified by Berg (1974) were proposed by this author as the primary educational focus of program. In order for the Committee to understand the meaning of the Twelve Techniques, a small group read Berg's (1972) materials and worked to redefine the techniques for possible programmatic use. Also, an audiovisual, *The Second Spring of Samantha Muffin,* was developed and proved to be a positive contribution to raising consciousness about the needs and possibilities of older persons as they seek renewal and fulfillment (Clark, 1975). The audiovisual was introduced in April of 1975 as a basic interpretative tool to assist members of the Center to understand the concepts of the Twelve Rejuvenating Techniques and to help prepare them for participating with meaning in an

Action/Investigation Project. *The Second Spring of Samantha Muffin* has been produced and is available through United Presbyterian Health Education and Welfare Department of the United Presbyterian Church in the U.S.A., together with a Study Guide.

The Steering Committee assumed responsibility for developing and conducting programs for experiencing and testing the Twelve Rejuvenating Techniques. The process included assignment of separate committees to deal with each technique, approval of programs submitted to the Steering Committee, presentation of programs to members of the Center, pre and post self-rating tests related to each technique, and evaluation of responses. A comprehensive test was given covering all Twelve Rejuvenating Techniques in an effort to measure the influence of the problems based on the Techniques in the lives of the participants in the Center. Briefly stated, the group's redefinition of the Twelve Techniques developed by Berg (1974), and the test responses based on programs related to the twelve different issues follow.

Remotivation

Apathy in older persons, often produced by isolation and loneliness, tends to cause them to replace persons and relationships with objects, and thus to lose alertness. Remotivation can be encouraged through the sharing of personal history, significant events, and common experiences. Relationships are discovered, established, and maintained through such sharing and can lead to further personal growth and involvement in society.

Only ten of the fifteen individuals chosen to be called on for remotivation were continued as study subjects, the others having refused contact with the volunteers or having been recommended as dropped from the project by the callers.

Responses on the pretests showed the majority of subjects lacked interest and social contact. There seemed, however, to be little depression, self-pity, or lack of self-esteem among respondents. Posttests revealed some improvement in interest and some increased social contact. Evidence of depression was not changed nor was self-pity. There seemed to be no change in the level of self-esteem. Three or four were very busy with other things. One was looking for a husband.

It was concluded that, of all the techniques, remotivation is the most difficult to use because it begins with a negative base. The persons who are believed to be in need of it have already withdrawn or otherwise lost the signs of active interest in life. When extrapolated on a large scale, the problem for our society is one of great magnitude. Prevention of this withdrawal would be much simpler than remotivation.

Physical Conditioning

Physical conditioning through adequate and regular exercise is basic to a sense of well-being. Older persons need assistance in discovering the kinds of exercise appealing and appropriate to them, and motivation to assure their use of such exercise.

Responses showed that the programs proved to be very helpful to most participants. There were some who were encouraged to see a doctor; many improved their eating habits and understanding of good nutrition. The importance of relaxation was appreciated and has become part of many respondents' regimen. In addition to responses of the tests, a number of expressions of recognition of the importance of physical conditioning were made during the project.

Education

Personal growth is a life-long need and process. Older persons retain the ability to learn. The elderly need to be made aware of and encouraged to use the multiple opportunities for adult education in their communities. The possibilities range from such general types of improvement as completing high school courses, learning new skills, teaching others, and courses for the sheer joy of learning. A few perceived needs are financial, nutrition, and health and safety education.

Responses to the tests showed that, indeed, there was general concern among the Center's members for survival education. The information they obtained through the programs focused their attention on basic survival issues. Members indicated they were helped most by programs on mental health, crime prevention, and safety. Respondents showed a very positive appreciation for the series.

Creative Resiliency
Positive mental attitude is basic to a satisfying life. It helps persons in becoming resilient, enabling them to rebound from loss or defeat.

Results from the tests indicated marked improvement in the attitude of the respondents in the area of handling crisis situations. There was a general feeling of capability to handle decisions and to bounce back from loss and problems. Individual and group sharing in the programs provided an opportunity for the exposure of needs and ways of meeting them.

Identification
The will to live is essential to a full life. While accepting the fact of aging, people need to be introduced to examples of older persons who are living life to the fullest by identifying with the spirit of life and power rather than of weakness.

Interest in volunteerism increased with the program emphases, according to testing records. Coupled with the interest, however, was a continuing need for further information about second careers. It is believed this area needs more interpretation and emphasis before respondents will show more interest. Members of the Center indicated a broad-scoped involvement in volunteer activity.

Acclimation to Death
The issue of death and dying confronts every person and is especially real to the elderly. The church is uniquely equipped and called to assist them in openly facing this reality so that they can be free to live creatively, confident that the promises of God about life now and beyond death are supportive and dynamic, and can help them live with courage and meaning and die with dignity and assurance.

Pretests showed most respondents felt they had dealt with matters relating to their death. Following the series there was an expression of definite change in feeling with positive steps taken by a significant number in preparation for death. Included were revised wills and funeral arrangements made.

Leisure Ethic
Older persons need help both in accepting their leisure without guilt and creatively using it. Giving of self for the well-being of others is a sign of fulfillment and the affirmation of life.

Most respondents felt good about leisure, as indicated on the pretests. The programs increased desire to improve the use of leisure time for most of the respondents. There seemed to be a feeling of change directly attributable to the emphases in the programs.

Spiritual Renewal
Spiritual renewal is essential to life fulfillment. The church has a special call to work with older persons toward this goal, recognizing the unlimited resources of the Christian faith for making life new. The strengthening of personal faith is a primary mission for the church and needs to be pursued with sensitivity, imagination, creativity, and persistence.

Posttests showed a general upswing in the feeling of importance of spiritual matters. After the series of programs, the majority of subjects were more positive about the importance of group sharing of spiritual problems and questions. Many were helped and wrote positive comments.

Community
Self-worth is closely related to a sense of independence, which was seen as a prized possession of every person. In the face of loss and change, older persons need reinforcement and assistance in maintaining their independence. Taking responsibility for their own lives through planning, creating, conducting, and participating in activities for themselves and others is basic to achieving and maintaining independence. The leadership potential in older persons is powerful and promising, although largely untapped, and must be acknowledged and employed.

Pretests showed a rather ambivalent awareness of community resources for older persons in San Diego. At the same time there was the desire for more information about such matters as housing, health, transportation, nursing care, and other available services.

Posttests revealed an almost unanimous acknowledgment and appreciation of new information gained. Of perhaps more significance was the report of more of a feeling of belonging to our community by knowing the resources available.

Preretirement Counseling

Retirement is one of the major transitions of life and is often traumatic. Preparation for this event encompassing the needs of the whole person is highly important and often makes the difference between successful retirement and the downhill slide into nothingness. Ideally, such counseling should begin as early as age thirty-five. The need to retire *to* something not *from* something is gaining acceptance.

In an all-day seminar, the majority of those in attendance indicated they had received help. Responses were positive with appreciation expressed for those who planned it. However, the evaluation showed a general feeling of great need for more preretirement counseling for those approaching that period of life.

United Action

The needs, problems, and possibilities of the aging are not limited to any one cultural, ethnic, economic, or religious group. Ecumenical and secular agencies can and must work together to create positive impact in meeting the common needs of older people to make aging a vital experience.

Tests showed that the concern of respondents changed from the need for better transportation to concern for crisis counseling, emergency food services, and nutritional assistance in their community. They also indicated a need for more social contact. There was a general feeling that united action is the best way to accomplish change, but respondents expressed ambivalence as to whether the Chatsworth Adult Center should become part of a larger group to join in united action.

Senior Power

Older persons are a vast national resource and are best equipped to take initiative for improving the image and conditions of life for senior citizens through action in political involvement. The church needs to encourage older persons to reach beyond themselves and lead in creating meaningful social roles for the elderly.

Pretests showed that respondents had a strongly positive feeling about the words "senior power." Tests also revealed feelings of respondents that they were not being adequately heard in matters pertaining to legislation and politics. There was an overwhelming interest expressed in learning more about what is being done by senior power advocates, and what members of the Center might do toward making a difference. Posttest results showed a definite increase of acceptance of each person's responsibility to bring about social change, beginning with a greater desire to express convictions on public matters through legislation.

Chatsworth Adult Center, having designed programs based on the Twelve Rejuvenating Techniques, believes they represent a holistic approach to the spiritual well-being of older persons and therefore are effective when used alone and together on a continuing basis. Having finished the Action/Investigation Project, expressions of leaders of the group have been that techniques will continue to be used for program planning, guidance, development, and evaluation.

Average attendance at meetings of the Chatsworth Adult Center has increased from six to over one hundred in the past three years. The greatest growth took place during the adventure in operationalizing the Twelve Rejuvenating Techniques. The Center continues to emit rays of hope and signs of help for older persons both in the church and the community. The word has spread through its members that something unique and strong is under way and that the door is open for any and all adults who wish to enter its life.

REFERENCES

Berg, K.P. *Senior power: New life for the church.* Unpublished doctoral dissertation, San Francisco Theological Seminary, 1974.

Clark, C. *The second spring of Samantha Muffin.* San Diego: United Presbyterian Health, Education and Welfare Association, 1975.

Leanse, J. & Wagner, S.P. *Directory of senior centers and clubs; A national resource.* Washington, D.C.: National Council on the Aging, Inc., 1974.

Maxwell, J.M. *Centers for older people.* Washington, D.C.: National Council on the Aging, Inc., 1962.

Chapter 21

FILIAL RESPONSIBILITY TO THE SENILE PARENT: A JEWISH PERSPECTIVE

LEVI MEIER

Guidelines for interpersonal relations are determined by Jewish law, which covers every life situation. For example, comforting the bereaved requires the comforter to be completely silent until the bereaved begins a conversation (Yoreh Deah 376:1). Similarly, the laws for visiting the sick require certain behavior, such as saying words of encouragement and helping the sick to arrange their financial affairs (Yoreh Deah 335:7).

Under ordinary circumstances, the behavior required for honoring one's father and mother is conceptually defined by two categories: honor and reverence (Kibbud and Morah). Honor is defined as positive acts of personal service. Rabbinic examples include feeding and dressing one's parent (Yoreh Deah 240:4). These examples illustrate that a child's relationship to his parent is comparable to that of a servant to his master. Reverence is defined as an avoidance of disrespectful acts. Rabbinic examples include not sitting in one's parents' seats, nor speaking before them and never contradicting them (Yoreh Deah 240:2). These examples demonstrate how, in general, a child should relate to his parents.

These child-parent obligations are applicable throughout the life-cycle: when the parents are young, middle-aged, and in their later period of life. The purpose of this chapter is to analyze whether these obligations are similarly applicable when one's parent is senile.

Senility does not refer to temporary forgetfulness or excessive reminiscing on the part of the aged parent. Senility, which is irreversible, is defined as chronic brain syndrome (Butler and

161

Lewis, 1973). Acute brain syndrome is reversible and does not fall in the category of senility. The mental status questionnaire devised by Kahn, Goldfarb, Pollack, and Peck (1960) clearly differentiates between acute and chronic brain syndrome.

Acute brain syndrome (ABS) differs from chronic brain syndrome in the areas of causes, symptoms, and treatment. For purposes of this discussion, symptoms and treatments are the most significant considerations. The symptoms of a reversible brain syndrome include a fluctuating level of awareness. The person typically is disoriented; recent memory is lost, while remote memory may be preserved. Restlessness or aggressiveness may appear in their behavior (Butler and Lewis, 1973; Libow, 1973; Verwoerdt, 1976).

The clinical symptoms of chronic brain syndrome (CBS) differ significantly from those of acute, reversible brain syndrome. There are two predominant types of chronic brain syndrome: senile psychosis and psychosis associated with cerebral arteriosclerosis.

The symptoms of senile psychosis may appear insidiously without any abrupt changes. Gradually, small differences in physical, mental, and emotional functioning are noticed. Early symptoms may include errors in judgment and decline in personal care and habits. Depression, anxiety, and irritability may also characterize the early stages of this syndrome. As the deterioration increases, the traditional five signs of organic dysfunction become more evident: disturbance and impairment of memory, impairment of intellectual functioning, impairment of judgment, impairment of orientation, and shallow or labile affect.

The symptoms of psychosis associated with cerebral arteriosclerosis can either be gradual or sudden. With a slower onset, there is usually a gradual intellectual loss, and impairment of memory tends to be spotty rather than complete. The course is up and down rather than progressively downhill (Butler & Lewis, 1973; Verwoerdt, 1976).

It appears that reversible brain syndrome can result in complete recovery once the person survives the physical crises that precipitated the psychiatric disorder. Treatment must be intensive but can often be short-term.

Senile psychosis is marked by steady and progressive deterioration and is eventually fatal. Emotional reactions may respond to treatment, and physical functioning can improve with proper support even though the physical loss is irreparable. Similarly, psychosis associated with cerebral arteriosclerosis can lead quickly to a fatal outcome or may produce an organic condition lasting a number of years.

In attempting to arrive at the Jewish law regarding care of a senile parent, one must rely not only on scientific definitions of brain syndromes, but also on the Talmudic treatment of mental dysfunction in a parent. An examination of some Talmudic passages may be instructive in attempting to determine the required behavior under Jewish law for dealing with one's senile parent. The Talmud asks the question, "How far does the honor of parents extend?" (Kiddushin 31a). A few Talmudic anecdotes would appear *prima facie* to indicate that if a parent behaves abnormally, the child's responsibility to honor his father or mother is not altered whatsoever. Rabbi Dimi gave this incident as an example: "Once he (Dama ben Netinah) was seated among the great men of Rome, dressed in a silken garment, when his mother came and tore the garment from him, slapped him on the head, and spat in his face—but he did not shame her" (p. 31a).

Rabbi Eliezer gives another example of how far one must go in honoring one's parent. "Till the father throws the wallet of the son into the sea, and his son does not shame him" (p. 32a).

These citations illustrate that even extreme deviations from normal parental behavior in no way alter the child's obligation to honor his parent, which remains an absolute, no matter what the difficulties of the child.

Maimonides (1178) codifies the two foregoing examples and establishes normative principles to guide people faced with similar circumstances.

How far must one go to honor one's father and mother? Even if they took his wallet full of gold pieces and threw it into the sea before his very eyes, he must not shame them, show pain before them, or display anger to them; but he must accept the decree of scripture and keep his silence. And how far must one go in his reverence? Even if he is dressed in precious clothes and is sitting in an honored place before many people, and his parents come and tear off his clothes, hitting him in the head and spitting in his face, he may not shame them, but he must keep silent, and be in awe and fear of the King of Kings who commanded him thus. For if a King of flesh and blood had decreed that he do something more painful than this, he could not hesitate in its performance. How much more so, then when he is commanded by Him who created the world at His will. (Mamrim 6:7)

Maimonides realizes the difficulties inherent in these events and in implementing these commandments. In his view, an additional motivation for the performance of these command- ments stems from one's fear of the King of Kings.

From these Talmudic anecdotes and from Maimonides' analy- sis of them, it would appear, as previously assumed, that if a parent behaves abnormally, the child's responsibility to honor his father or mother is not altered whatsoever. On the contrary, one finds that the child's responsibility increases in direct proportion to the specific needs of his parents. Also, as at any other time, personal service (honor) and the abstinence from disrespect (reverence) must characterize dealings with a parent in such a situation.

In addition to the codification of these two examples, Maimonides establishes a separate category for the conduct required in dealing with one's mentally disturbed parent. Mai- monides writes: "If one's father or mother should become mentally disordered, he should try to treat them as their mental state demands, until they are pitied by God. But if he finds he cannot endure the situation because of their extreme madness, let him leave and go away, deputing others to care for them properly" (Mamrim 6:10).

There is no Talmudic discussion on this topic cited by Maimonides as his basis for this codification. However, com- mentaries on Maimonides assume that the following anecdote is the basis for his statement: "Rabbi Assi had an aged mother. Said she to him, 'I want ornaments.' So he made them for her. 'I want a husband as handsome as you.' Thereupon he left her and went to Palestine" (Kiddushin 31b).

The departure of Rabbi Assi from Babylon has been interpreted as an acceptable response to the action of his senile mother. Rabbi

Assi, unable to respond to his aged, senile mother in a constructive manner, leaves her in Babylon and makes his way to Palestine.

Maimonides' codification accentuates three essential points, as Blidstein (1975) points out: the parent is classified as mentally disturbed; the son is exempt from personal service to his parent, but not from the responsibility to see to it that others attend to it; and, the point of the son's exemption from personal service to his senile parent is the son's own evaluation of the situation.

Maimonides clearly does more than just codify this Talmudic event. He elucidates, explicates, and adds some interpretive dimensions. For example, the Talmud does not mention that the child is responsible for seeing to it that parental care is delivered by someone else.

The Rabad (1193) argues with Maimonides' conclusion and states: "This is an incorrect teaching. If he leaves, whom will he assign to watch his parent?" (Gloss, Mamrim 6:10). The Rabad maintains that there is no limitation to the son's responsibility. However, Maimonides' statement was codified in the Shulhan Arukh and is, therefore, to be understood as normative Judaism.

The basic question arising from Maimonides' citations centers on his differentiation betwen a parent's acting abnormally (Mamrin 6:7) and his being mentally disturbed (*Nitrefa da'ato*, Mamrin 6:10). Whereas abnormal parental behavior must be withstood by a son, care of a mentally disturbed parent may be delegated to others.

The examples of parental behavior given by the Talmud, throwing one's son's wallet in the sea and tearing his clothes in front of dignitaries, in contrast to saying "I want a husband as handsome as you," are not in themselves sufficient for differentiating between abnormal behavior and mental disturbance.

The key issue in these quotations is the halachically acceptable response to these problems. In Mamrin 6:7, the son must tolerate abnormal parental behavior. However, in Kiddushin (31b), as codified by Maimonides in Mamrin 6:10, Rabbi Assi is allowed to depart for Palestine, leaving care of his aged mother to others.

One suggested explanation for these two distinct halachic codifications by Maimonides may be that he equates Rabbi Assi's mother's condition with a chronic, irreversible brain syndrome, while he regards the examples in Mamrin 6:7 as cases of temporary abnormality.

The categories of honor and reverence apply in the cases of every normal and abnormal parental behavior but may be suspended in cases of behavior that results from permanent mental disturbance. Even extreme deviations from the norm and totally illogical behavior on the part of parents must be tolerated when that behavior is the result of an acute condition, such as an acute brain syndrome. In these cases, filial responsibility increases according to parental needs. In these situations, constructive responses can be expected since the situation is reversible.

However, a chronic brain syndrome, an irreversible condition, falls into a different category. The Torah recognizes the possibility that the children may reach their tolerance level; it, therefore, exempts them from direct personal service. However, the responsibility to see to it that someone else takes care of their parents is incumbent upon them.

Blidstein's (1975) brilliant analysis of the commandment to honor one's parents fails to comment on the interrelationship between the Maimonides codification of Mamrin 6:7 and Mamrin 6:10. Similarly, he does not differentiate between chronic and acute brain syndrome.

Only with an understanding of the distinction between these two types of brain syndrome can different filial responses towards abnormal parental behavior be understood. Naturally, every deviation from the parental norm must initially be treated as acute until evidence indicates that the condition is in fact irreversible. Chronic brain syndrome may be a legitimate reason for transferring the obligation for attentiveness to the needs of the parents to others. Old age and the normal infirmities that may accompany it do not provide sufficient reason for transferring this obligation. Old age is expected to stimulate additional contact between parent and offspring rather than abandonment of the parent.

This hypothesis concerning the differentiation between acute and chronic brain syndrome in determining the applicable Jewish law may be supported by an additional citation from Maimonides' codification. He not only distinguishes between abnormal behavior (Mamrin 6:7) and behavior due to mental disturbance (Mamrin 6:10), but he also hints indirectly at a distinction between chronic (Mamrin 6:10) and acute brain syndrome (Mamrin 6:7).

Maimonides stipulates that every mental disturbance must be initially dealt with until filial tolerance is exhausted due to the parents' extreme condition. This condition must be chronic and, therefore, irreversible. An acute brain syndrome, although very taxing, will not worsen, but will, indeed, improve significantly when dealt with. In such a situation, filial responsibility is not suspended.

One might point to the Midrash's comment (Deuteronomy 1:15) on the incident of Dama ben Netinah, "His mother was mentally disturbed," as contradicting Maimonides and the Shulhan Arukh, since they categorize this incident as one demanding filial responsibility. It may be that they based their rulings on the understanding that if the mother were mentally disturbed, it was an acute condition, or, perhaps, they disregarded this version of the event and just assumed the mother's behavior to be an extreme deviation from the norm.

All human relationships are guided by normative prescription, thereby actualizing the limitless potential man possesses to imitate God. Age is a blessing. Concomitantly with the aging process are related situations that require our serious attention. Honoring one's parents deserves a central place within this scheme.

REFERENCES

Blidstein, G. *Honor thy father and mother.* New York: Ktav Publishing House, 1975.

Butler, Robert N., & Lewis, Myrna I. *Aging and mental health: Positive psychosocial approaches.* St. Louis: C.V. Mosby Co., 1973.

Deuteronomy Rabbah 1:15, as quoted by Tosafot Kiddushin 31a, s.v. 'u-ba'at.

Kahn, R.L., Goldfarb, A.I., Pollack, M., & Peck, A. Brief objective measures for the determination of mental status in the aged. *American Journal of Psychiatry,* 1960, *117,* 326-328.

Karo, Joseph. Yoreh Deah, *Shulhan Arukh.*

Kiddushin, the Babylonian Talmud. Translated by G. Blidstein, *Honor thy father and mother.* New York: Katv Publishing House, 1975.

Libow, Leslie S. Pseudo-senility: Acute and reversible organic brain syndromes. *Journal of the American Geriatrics Society*, 1973, *21*, 112-120.

Maimonides, Moses. *The code of Maimonides.* Translated by A. Hershman. New Haven: Yale Judaica Series.

Rabad, Abraham ben David, Glosses in the Maimonidean Code, 1193.

Verwoerdt, Adriaan. *Clinical geropsychiatry.* Baltimore: Williams and Wilkins, 1976.

Chapter 22

PASTORAL INTERVENTION WITH THE TERMINALLY ILL

GREGORY L. JACKSON

The pastor is often portrayed in the literature on death as a cultic functionary who merely performs the last rites of passage before burial. Attempts to describe the minister's role in a more positive light have not been adequate.

Kastenbaum and Aisenberg (1976), for example, quote Buxbaum with evident approval: "It is the task of the pastor, and that which makes him so valuable a resource to the busy hospital personnel, to be there for no other reason than simply to *be with* the patient" (p. 186). If the minister's job is limited to such passivity, however, then the unique and crucial role that can be performed by the clergy in death situations is lost, and no other professional can fill the void. Unlike the doctor, nurse, or social worker, the pastor often has the ability to intervene in a family situation in order to promote the emotional and spiritual welfare of individuals. A case study of a man's last five days of life may illustrate some of the qualities of pastoral intervention.

Death at Home

Roger Olson was known by his friends for his unusual vigor as well as for his shortness of breath. People worried about his health but did not expect him to die. On December 8 he was taken by ambulance to the hospital, unconscious. His wife was tormented by two notions: that he might not live, and that he might suffer a state of protracted dying. She called the three children, all grown and married and living elsewhere. On December 10, Roger came home to his family with an oxygen tank. The diagnosis was severe emphysema. Recovery would mean being able to walk only to and from the television. The pastor, who knew the family well, discussed the situation at length with Regina and the children, and finally with Roger, who did not wish to use the oxygen. On December 12 the son and his wife left. Roger was feeling better. The family called the pastor later in the afternoon. Roger said he felt wonderful, "I have been using too much oxygen. I feel light-headed." He in fact was much worse. The pastor said, "Perhaps you are dying." Roger did not want any measures taken. The pastor gave him communion and prayed with him. The pastor called in the family members to speak about their grief, since no one knew whether Roger would live another day or year. Roger spoke to each privately and to all of them together. The son had already said in the morning, "Dad, I probably won't see you again." Roger sat in his favorite chair in the bedroom and slipped into a coma. He died around 4:00 AM the next day, December 13, surrounded by his family in a calm, loving atmosphere.

Intervention

An elaboration of this case will illustrate the repeated opportunities for the minister to act as a catalyst, offer support, supply information, serve as mediary, and focus the family's attention on the reality and religious meaning of this death in their lives. The dynamics of certain family members in those five days supports the argument that the minister's role is active rather than passive, and that it is unique and essential.

Regina was at the hospital on December 8 when the pastor arrived. She was in an agitated state but displayed a remarkable degree of discernment about what this meant. They had lived in a state of denial for years, with Roger ignoring the state of his health and all of the family colluding in this process to some degree. She had participated in a church seminar on death at the local funeral home. She had seen her mother horribly disfigured by cancer of the brain. Regina was brave but also was uncertain about the use of heroic measures to preserve life or, perhaps, to prolong death. The minister went to Roger's room with Regina and prayed with her. She was at a loss as to what to do. She did not want to alarm the children and did not wish to keep them in the dark. The minister said, "Roger may die. We can tell that just by listening to his labored breathing. Your children will probably want to come. This is a kind of death, facing Roger's critical condition. If he lives, you will all have to face a new type of life."

Regina called the children, all of whom decided to come to the family home with their spouses. It was to be several hours before the first arrived, so the minister waited and drank coffee with Regina. They spoke of the pros and cons of hospital treatment for terminal cases. The Quinlan case was discussed. It was decided that the decision was one to be shared by Roger, the family, and the doctor. The minister spoke of the dangers of suppressing grief and the healing that comes with accepting the harshest reality of life. Regina understood from her own experience that this was so. The result of the session was to prepare her for a difficult time, in which she would lose the most yet bear the greatest burden in helping the children and relatives.

After some sleep the minister visited Roger at the hospital on December 9 and spoke with him about the gravity of the illness and the family's concern. Regina had warned him that Roger would not want to worry his family by admitting how sick he was. They in turn would not want to disturb him because of their concern for his feelings. This was, of course, a perfect setting for self-perpetuating denial. The minister went to the family home and spoke with everyone, since all had arrived during the night. Roger was better, but the tests would show that he was terribly impaired. No one could say what would happen. The tension was overwhelming. The minister asked how everyone felt about the future and was asked for his own opinion. He said, "I am not a medical person, so my judgments are practical in nature. Roger may die today," The subject was changed immediately. He went on, "Roger may also linger for years. I have seen sudden death in healthy people and I have witnessed protracted death in the frailest ninety-year-old woman. We need to deal with both alternatives." The minister went on to insist on honesty with Roger, even if it had to be gradual, and suggested that they consider what they might do in terms of heroic measures. The family began to speak of where Regina would live, if Roger lived or if he died. They anxiously asked if preparations should be made. The minister said, "It seems callous, but it means facing reality. Being prepared will not hurt, no matter what happens."

On Friday, December 10, the minister again went to the family home, where Roger by this time had been moved. The oxygen tank in the living room was an ominous sign of the change in their lives. Roger was in his chair in the bedroom. He did not wish to use the oxygen. The minister spoke to him. Roger displayed what has been called middle knowledge (Weisman, 1976). He was aware of the problems but also rather detached.

In the living room, the minister conveyed the message to the family they could talk about impending death. Alice, the youngest daughter, who was also pregnant, left and went to the kitchen. The other children and Regina agreed that Roger would not want to be hospitalized again. He had worked almost to the day of his most recent attack. He was an active man who did not wish to be doomed to a life on the couch watching soap operas and game shows. The family was prepared to begin speaking of their grief with Roger, but everyone was worried about the bottled-up emotion in Alice, who was vomiting in the kitchen. They were concerned for the effect upon the unborn child as well. Alice avoided going in "the room." She was extremely tense. The minister said he would intervene.

The minister began to speak with Alice. She moved through three rooms before he stopped her at the stairway. "Alice, your father knows he could soon die. He wants to speak to you. You know it will help, as hard as it is." He placed his arm around her shoulder and guided her into the bedroom. She knelt on the floor, unable to speak. The minister said, "Alice knows that you might never see her first child. She wants to tell you what you mean to her, but it is hard." Roger said, as Alice wept and held him, "I know, Alice. We understand each other." The minister left the room and let them speak. The fear of grief and honesty faded as the family helped each other.

The anticipatory grief made the last day one of extraordinary calm in the midst of crisis. After Roger had communion and refused oxygen once again, the family members came in at different times to be with him, to say goodbye, to cry. He drifted into a coma or sleep in the afternoon, awakening somewhat with a startled look twice, saying, "Oh. You're still here!" The minister spent time in the bedroom with different members of the family and also went to the living room. They spoke about what death is like. Roger breathed with difficulty and seemed to worsen. Practical questions were answered in the living room. The minister called the funeral director. The family planned a simple service and suggested hymns and readings, shared personal insights and memories. The minister left late in the evening, no great change being visible. Roger died in his favorite chair in the bedroom at some time that night.

Although the funeral is often described as that point in which grief begins, it has greater meaning when the bereaved have already had a chance to begin the growth and healing that emerges from the grief process. When the minister has actively shared in that evolution, he may integrate his service with the experience of the family, speaking to the inner circle who grieve the most, while also addressing the more distant friends and relatives, who arrive with the feelings of shock, denial, and dismay that the others have left behind. The service and especially the sermon deal, then, with the situation of the mourners as they accept a death and a new life within their religious framework. It is not the beginning of grief for the family, and the graveside service does not end the period of mourning. The intervention of the minister continues as he visits the family members after the swarm of friends and relatives have left the spouse and children alone. He visits the family to remind them that the loss was real, that a new life needs to be created, that the pain of loss is not transformed in a month or a year. When grief is acute, he may say that the agony will abate and peaceful memories will bring smiles instead of tears.

Theological Perspective and Problems

The Christian faith began with death and the reinterpretation of that death for the followers of Christ. The concept and reality of eternal life does not inform the believer unless the mask of denial is removed. The theology of the cross in the epistles of Paul and the writings of Luther confront the minister with the origin of Christianity in suffering, shame, and death. In dealing with cases of terminal illness, the minister must realize that he is not helpless or powerless. The hospital and the home are open to him. The conscientious funeral director will work with him. The doctor will advise him. The family will ask for information and sources of information. The minister is engaged in some of the most important work of all in the death of an individual. He addresses himself as Nighswonger (1972) has said, to certain pain of death, ·the religious perception of suffering in a land that denies its reality, the emotional development and material needs of the families for whom he is reponsible. It demands that he be informed about the whole realm of death and dying, that he face his own mortality and his own resistance to such a thought, and that he grow with families in their spiritual development and understanding.

Mills (1969) has said that the minister has the obligation to affirm what the community ignores, that all must die, that everyone must deal with others and with themselves in grief situations. The minister should conduct educational seminars to inform the community and encourage the proper conduct of morticians in dealing with the bereaved. The minister has not lost his power or authority, but he has often given it up without a whimper.

In the case described, the previous knowledge of Regina enabled her to choose a funeral director who emphasized service rather than glitter and unctiousness.

The mortician did not pressure the widow and family to go beyond their limits. This case is fortuitous because of the strength of the family, the wisdom of the doctor, the perception of the wife, the support of church members, and the respect all felt for Roger. The argument, therefore, is not that the minister occupied a new role, but rather that he filled the one appropriate to him as a pastor and not to anyone else. The function of the minister is heightened when he is fully engaged in the complex events of a person's last days.

REFERENCES

Katenbaum, R., & Aisenberg, R. *The psychology of death, concise edition.* New York: Springer Publishing Company, 1976.
Mills, L. Pastoral care of the dying and the bereaved. In L. Mills (Ed.) *Perspectives on death.* Nashville: Abingdon Press, 1969.
Nighswonger, C. Ministry to the dying as a learning encounter. *Journal of Pastoral Care,* 1972, *26*, 86-92.
Weisman, A. Denial and middle knowledge. In E. Scneidman (Ed.), *Death: Current perspectives.* Palo Alto: Mayfield Publishing Company, 1976.

Section V

SPIRITUAL WELL-BEING IN RELATION TO THE ENVIRONMENT

SPIRITUAL WELL-BEING OF THE ELDERLY IN RELATION TO THE ENVIRONMENT

Daniel M. Munn

This chapter was inspired by a bumper sticker that said, "What do you want to be when you grow old?" I am interested in that because I am interested in preparing a place for myself; I think that answering the question posed in the bumper strip will also speak to the issue of spiritual well-being of the elderly in relation to the environment.

What do I envision that I will be as old? More wise, I hope. More ignorant, I presume. I want to be financially secure. To continue to grow in wisdom and stature, in favor with God and man.

At age forty-two, I wonder what do I fear about old age? I fear not being needed, that there will be no role for me. I fear not being in control, not master of my fate. I fear being isolated. Where will my children be in this mobile society? Will I be out of touch with life? I fear dependence, being a burden to others. I fear being sick, or even worse, boring. I fear I will not know what to do with leisure.

With these data of what I imagine myself to be or what I fear will happen, I begin to see an image of an environment or a milieu that I can both appreciate and affect. My environment will have education, to help me in my retirement. It will have health care, particularly an emphasis on preventive health care. It will have the availability of natural surroundings, if some fool has not yet asphalted the whole of Yosemite. It will have the opportunity for friendly contacts, preferably of all ages, and resources for intellectual and physical activity. In short, I want an environment that lets me be.

What is first and foremost is there must be meaning. If I am

179

going to fit into an environment, there must be a place for me. Of course, there is much spiritual growth to be had in adjusting to not being wanted, or being transformed from a person into a non-person by the remarkable feat of passing a birthday. I know that biologic deterioration is not so much to be feared as the loss of interest.

These individualistic goals will never substitute for the knowledge that the people among whom I am going to spend my last years know my name, all of them of all ages. My name. A powerful biblical term for my very being in the world. If God should forget my name, I would cease that moment to exist. We who are created in His image have similar power. We can name and unname with awesome power. A friend of mine used to say, "Sticks and stones will break my bones but names will kill me." One of the greatest challenges for the churches and synagogues in our country today is to provide a name for our old ones. This is the environment that needs the most attention. It is the ecological imbalance most threatening to man because it attacks the soul.

Of what use is a human being who has passed that phase of life our society deems most valuable, the productive and reproductive phase? How do you grow in the acceptance of your limitations? What is it like to watch what you valued so much slip away, from physical prowess to friends and loved ones? Is a gentle, loving, involved detachment in the world possible? Do you learn easier ways to shift priorities?

One of the dangers that I see looming is that elderly people will become the next service project of the eager religious population, as if being old was the problem. The problem is our attitude. We have done that sort of thing before, you know. We have done it with premarital counseling, with sex manuals, and most recently we risk forcing persons to die with dignity whether they want to or not.

We need to change. We, the people who claim to love the Lord, are the environment most conducive to wholeness to our aging brothers and sisters and, indeed, to ourselves. We are in fact the spiritual dimension. The purpose, the meaning, the neededness of older people is ours to define and live. No amount of material provision will substitute for the family of God naming each and every member of the family as worthwhile in every phase of life's journey right to the end.

Chapter 24

SURVIVORSHIP AND SPIRITUAL STRENGTH: PRECEPTS OF THE HOLOCAUST FOR AGING AND OLD AGE

Shoshana Avner

Aging and survivorship assume functional equivalence throughout the lifespan of the individual. Exponential significance is assigned to survivorship in old age. It may be perceived as a reward; as a sign of favor by the diety; as a stroke of luck; as salvation; as the logical, expected culmination of a lifetime of personal discipline; or as the destiny of a population grouping.

We are all survivors, as we age throughout the life cycle. For many older people, survivorship becomes a full-time occupation. One need only observe or converse with septuagenarians or octogenarians to assess the significance of survival—simply, the fact of life after others' demise. Days of birth are juxtaposed with days of death or memory in competition with one's age cohort.

Why is survivorship important to older people? Younger people seem to take it for granted, even when unexpected tragedy strikes in the form of the death of a peer or an older person. Time, a formerly limitless resource, becomes a scarce resource to the aged. Others' mortality is a constant reminder, ever more frequent and insistent with advancing age.

One's formula for survivorship assumes a high element of idiosyncracy, sheer pragmatism, and familiarity of habit. If there is no fountain of youth; if cosmetology and transplant technology have circumscribed boundaries; if notions of an afterlife have limited appeal in a space-age world; if religious institutions have low salience and relevance for a post-Holocaust, post-Hiroshima, post-Viet Nam, post-Watergate world; then, why bother with survivorship? Why strive for longevity, why endure, why persist, why continue? The glorification of retirement leisure assumes Pyrrhic proportions for many older people—particularly with the constant lowering of retirement age for ever-healthier, better educated, more affluent, and more sophisticated adults.

What are the implications for daily life through the years? If one looks to conditions of extremity for clues and directions, is it possible to transmit and adapt such strategies for life to psychosocial devastations in one's personal life contingency repertoire? How did the Holocaust survivors do it? How could they do it? What makes the difference? Even as we keep their memory hallowed in life, we can make the humble attempt to reach out to integrate their unbelievable experiences and to understand the awesome insights of victims and survivors alike.

In his remarkable book on death camp survivors, Terrence Des Pres (1976) defines survival as the capacity to sustain terrible damage in mind and body and yet to be there, sane, alive, and still human. He sees a survivor as anyone trying to keep life and spirit intact. Fixed activities seem to have been the most significant factor in the struggle for survival. These included forms of social bonding and interchange, collective resistance, keeping one's dignity and moral sense active.

Des Pres speaks of dignity as an inward resistance to determination by external forces, a sense of autonomy. The individual who would survive could not afford to lose a sense of dignity. At some point, it became necessary to resist the steady obliteration of the self as a human being.

Heroism is not a grand gesture or glory, nor is it dramatic defiance of superior individuals. The survivor manages to stay alive, in body and spirit, without the loss of will in human terms, despite the dread and hopelessness that must be endured. It is a fight to live that matters, not the manner of death. Bare survival is not enough. The individual needs to come through as a living soul in a living body, beyond despair and self-pity. One chooses to live, to live humanly, to have faith in life.

There is a special dignity and clearness of vision to those existing under conditions of outward helplessness and victimization. The ordeal of survival becomes an experience of growth and purification. The struggle to live humanly involves the process of becoming more human because of extraordinary demands of extreme living conditions.

Surviving and bearing witness are reciprocal acts; bearing witness becomes a goal. A mutual pact is drawn that anyone who survives and becomes free must speak out on behalf of the others. Thus, the survivor transcends death, somehow, as well as the helplessness that destroyed hope and self-respect. The will to bear witness becomes a survivor "task," part of an ego ideal.

It is clear that survivorship involves intelligence in several different meanings: mental powers, sagacity, acumen, calculating shrewdness, espionage, reconnaissance, inspection, a survey of one's environment regarding its possibilities, limitations, and dangers. It is a military posture, an adversary stance relative to one's surroundings. It requires vigilance and powers of observation regarding major trends and minutiae over a long period of time.

After all is said and done, what fueled people to survive the ghastly environment of the Holocaust? Why would anyone want to survive under those conditions of living death or deathly life? Survival motivation involved a sense of obligation for one's own life and the survival of the community, especially strong in Judaism. This tradition is incumbent on each individual, on an active basis, in one's personal life and in communal life. Another motivation was the need for continuity of self and family, a sense of personal mission to immortalize one's selfhood, directly or indirectly, through one's natural family or through an adopted, extended family. Also, there must have been an acceptance of God's will, a notion of orderliness and rationality to the universe, a delegation of meaning to all actions as expressions of God's purpose, though not always known to us.

How do we relate these motivations for survival and resistance to aging and old age? It must be obvious that survivors are active resistors who function in a social matrix, whatever the survival motivation or the mode of resistance. Abraham Heschel (1959) put it very well: "The way to pure intention is paved with good deeds" (p. 404) and "It is the act, life itself, that educates the will. The good motive comes into being while doing the good" (p. 405).

Above all, the basic existential decision of life, affirmation, must be made. An individual must decide that life is worth living, despite multiple, simultaneous changes and significant losses, or that it is not.

Essentially, mechanisms of survival rest on an economic model; that is, the availability and distribution of resources. An interlocking resource system is attainable only on an accrual basis, through preparation of a personal resource bank with respect to inner resources: physical, economic, and social. One can draw only on lifetime rights from this resource portfolio, on a personal and collective contributory basis. Essentially, it is a model of scarcity, for the most precious resource, time, is at a premium.

Holocaust survivors depended upon a variety of strategies for continuity of life, whether singly or in combination. At times, acceptance of powerlessness or submission may be functional for survival purposes. Yet, the mobilization of anger about injustice, resistance to evil, of social action and political involvement may prove to be the single motivating, life-giving thrust. Realistic confrontation of reality, self-reliance, a search for the best potentialities, and sheer audacity can be very effective resources throughout life.

The choice of life, the decision that one shall live, one must live, is a critical one. Individuals living under fairly similar circumstances may have quite disparate lifespans, simply on the basis of this decisional outcome. The critical factors include a will to live, stubbornness in the face of obstacles, discipline, awareness of death, and the assignment of moral meaning to a living survival.

The consciousness of choice and the importance of struggle toward the attainment of worthwhile ends to guide one's destiny as a survivor all figure in the choice to live humanly, without compromises.

This risk-benefit analysis may be performed in the privacy of one's thoughts or in concert with others, who may harbor similar questions. Whatever the setting or process, it is a logical, rational, systematic decisional process. There are no illusions in confronting this difficult choice, the keystone of a choice system. Its power rests on its diagnostic function. Help resources can be mobilized as necessary.

An ideology, cause, or social movement may appeal to individuals for whom God is dead, as happened with many Holocaust survivors. Very few continued to trust in God, to hope for the best. Perhaps those who opted for reliance on chance or impulse were mystics, in their own way, trusting to a higher divine justice in the guise of luck. Some older people refer to their "traitorship" to religious institutions as a result of narcissism and dissatisfaction with change of major traditions. Others point to the difficulty in reinstituting the break in traditional affil- iation, because of changes in family composition.

Conclusion

Religious institutions, however, have a central and significant role to play with the expanding population of older adults. Their potential can be realized by focusing on the needs, interests, and wants of older adults. For too long, religion has segregated itself from the ongoing daily concerns of every man or every woman. A parochial, constricting view of function and role has resulted. The spotlight needs to shift from religious institutions' concerns and theological definitions of religiosity to human needs toward survival on human and humane terms. We cannot assume integration of older adults in congregational life simply because young and old come together for specific purposes for a few hours a week.

Religious institutions can be in the forefront and the center of community life. They can initiate, develop, and support pro- grams designed to foster life. They can be the vanguard of value systems that give strength in the development and survival of older persons. They can provide a myriad of opportunities for older people to bond in innovative ways, so that we need not fear old age.

REFERENCES

Des Pres, T. *The survivor: An anatomy of life in the death camps.* New York: Oxford University Press, 1976.
Heschel, A.J. *God in search of man.* New York: JPS-Meridian, 1959.

Chapter 25

RELIGION IN THE REHABILITATION OF THE AGED

EDITH ABRAAMS

Since so many institutional residents are vey old and frail, there is an increasing need to develop more meaningful activities if institutional settings are to prove to be more than custodial. This chapter describes a demonstration program attempted at the Hebrew Rehabilitation Center for Aged in Boston, Massachusetts.

Like many similar homes and hospitals for the chronically ill and brain-damaged aged, the institution functions as a residential facility and chronic disease hospital. Most residents will never return to community living. Rehabilitation is defined by the mutli-disciplinary staff as the maximum utilization of remaining physical, mental, emotional, and social capacities of individuals and possible prevention of further deterioration. Although the admissions policy is open, the population has been Jewish, with the majority originating from Eastern Europe.

The rehabilitation program described occurred over a period of one and one-half years on a forty-bed unit housing the most physically and mentally deteriorated men, eighty to one hundred years old. About one-half of the men were considered mentally alert, and the mental confusion of the others varied from mild to severe. Although the physical surroundings were bright and cheerful, and medical and nursing care provided was superior, a mood of deep apathy and depression pervaded. Many seemed oblivious to their surroundings and sat with eyes closed, heads resting on their chests. Transfer to this unit was often considered by resident and family as punishment rather than for the intended purposes of maximum care. Some staff even referred to it as "Siberia."

One wondered how these men could be energized and by what meaningful activity. It seemed doubtful that much could be done on a one-to-one casework basis, but perhaps a group program might work. Most of these men were from Eastern Europe and had in common a knowledge of the Hebrew prayers and rituals. Mark Zborowski and Elizabeth Herzog (1952) state: "According to the *shtetl* (small town of Eastern Europe) the children of Israel have survived solely because of the covenant made with God in accepting his law" (p. 30). Could religion, perhaps, be the spark to rekindle some meaningful activity?

The point, however, was not to impose religious practice, but to try to reawaken memories of ceremonies from earlier days. The Hebrew Rehabilitation Center has always had an ongoing religious program for the more than sixty-five years of its existence, but it has always been held in the synagogue located on the main floor.

It was discovered that three men were devout and prayed regularly each morning upon arising in their rooms, as they were unable to travel unaided to the synagogue. Asked if they would like to attend a Friday night service, for a time volunteers escorted these men. Unfortunately, this effort was unsuccessful. Although appreciative, one was unequal to the distance of the long corridors, another disrupted the service by moving about the large auditorium, and the third wandered about bewildered. However, he was aware he was experiencing a religious service and with much emotion, took my hand and murmured: "God bless you."

These initial reactions caused me to question whether the environment could be manipulated to eliminate these problems. Could services be brought to the men in their own unit? I then began to explore with them the idea of their having religious services in their own recreational lounges. Some of the men who had been inactive for so long were apathetic to the proposal, but a number expressed enthusiasm. However, when the then Center rabbi was consulted, he indicated a preference that those who wished could attend his service in the synagogue. Nevertheless, I continued exploring this possibility and received approval from the Director of Social Service, the Director of Nursing, and the Unit Charge Nurse. The Administration authorized the purchase of additional prayer books, prayer shawls, skull caps, and an electric lectern to amplify the weak voices of the men in conducting their service. The former physician-in-chief, who also happened to be a Hebraic scholar, advised on the portions of the service to be included.

Cooperation was solicited from the nursing and housekeeping service on the unit to ensure that the lounge area was always clean, the men properly attired, and that jackets and ties were worn, although some attended in pajamas and bathrobe. If the very confused were in their gerichairs, they were not removed from the room unless they became disruptive. To the questions posed by the men on the propriety of praying in pajamas or the feasibility of including the mentally confused, I invariably would reply: "God doesn't care about the outside of a person; to pray might help." Initially, some men needed repeated reassurance of being welcome, but soon felt certain of reception and relaxed. Within a few weeks twelve to eighteen men came regularly and promptly. A few months later several women from the adjoining unit were invited to join, and a few of the men enjoyed calling for and returning them to their quarters.

This abbreviated service was scheduled for 10:00 AM and 4:00 PM. The regularity of time provided a secure structure for resocialization. A resident claimed he had once been a cantor and volunteered to lead the service. Almost immediately the men expressed their displeasure with his unmelodious voice and poor Hebrew pronunciation and requested a replacement. This was the first sign of group feeling. I recalled having been moved by the beautiful chanting of a ninety-five-year-old man who sat in the corner of his room repeating continuously the daily worship service. Since he was blind, I asked if he would be willing to chant for the group assisted by another resident. The latter, a former sexton, sat by his side in the lounge and guided him through the touch of the hand or an appropriate phrase. The residents appreciated his melodious chants. I made a tape of his voice, which was used on the days he was unable to be with the group.

The goal was to have as much resident participation in the service as possible, to give each participant a sense of achievement. Residents took turns in reciting prayers, either from memory or the prayer book, or leading in the hymn singing.

Others looked forward to the rewards of praise and occasionally a sample packet of cigarettes given for distributing and collecting the prayer books, shawls, and skull caps.

A group feeling developed as these services deepened. Men became more interested in each other. They reported teaching and learning, at night, the procedures of the service that had been forgotten. As memories of the past were evoked, men expressed great satisfaction in "holding the prayer book in my hands after 30 or 40 years" and early childhood experiences of accompanying their fathers to the synagogue. Memories were evoked also of their past absorption in work and family. One of the men expressed hs gratitude by presenting me with an embroidered black velvet skull cap, which he had asked his son to purchase, as a reward for being "a leader of our people." This I wore each day to the service.

Part of the ritual is reading from the Holy Scriptures on Monday, Thursday, and Saturday mornings. One of the synagogue leaders agreed to do the reading for the group on Thursday mornings. Following this service and when ushering in the Sabbath on Friday afternoon, Kiddush, the tradition of serving wine or whisky with cake or cookies, was also observed. Volunteers usually assisted with the Kiddush.

The group's total emotional involvement and cohesiveness was shown when one of its members, aged ninety-six years, lost his forty-year-old son. Everyone attended the daily morning and afternoon service for the traditional thirty-day mourning period. One could feel the flow of sympathy and sharing of grief as the father led the prayers, sobbing. A deeply reverent and intense empathy was evident. Edgar N. Jackson (1965) states: "It is important that the bereaved person have a safe framework within which he can express all the feelings that are set in motion by the loss of the beloved. The ritualized religious expression does this by releasing the emotional responses that grow from group need and group support" (p. 224).

The men seemed comfortable about saying the Kadish in unison on the death of a group member, and when the resident we had taped died, they mourned him, expressing the loss of a loved one. Some of the men were able to talk about their readiness to die "when the time comes, but, hopefully, without suffering." By sharing in the open expression of mourning, perhaps they were doing some preparatory grief work in anticipation of their own death.

The services helped improve family relationships. Visiting children and grandchildren made a point of attending, becoming part of the group service, and were deeply moved. Tears were noted in a daughter's eyes as her father hobbled with his walker to the lectern to say a prayer from memory. Grandchildren were amazed that grandparents with severe short-term memory loss could still recite prayers and sing traditional melodies. After one resident with a severe asthmatic condition finished leading a morning service, he rushed to the phone to report his accomplishment to his son. A man previously considered noisy and belligerent now seemed to have attained some inner stability as he acted more reasonably with his family, other residents, and staff.

Staff cooperation was vital. Although initially some nurses protested the extra work involved, later these same nurses were observed sitting encouragingly next to a frail individual, holding a prayer book or straightening a prayer shawl. When the service was occasionally cancelled, the charge nurse often remonstrated: "The men want their service. They need it."

When the environment on this unit became more alive, nursing, housekeeping, and medical staff became enthusiastic, the unit internist even asking if similar programming could be developed for the adjoining female unit to "improve their quality of life." On that unit a regular weekly Friday afternoon service of blessing the candles ushering in the Sabbath was started by another member of the social service staff who eventually was able to motivate as many as thirty of the forty female residents to participate. Although many were completely disoriented, they could recall from memory the prayer of blessing the candles as they took turns in the group, often sharing their colorful scarves used in covering their heads during the prayer. During the Kiddush of wine and cookies that followed, they often reminisced about Friday night with their families in their own homes.

After about a year of ongoing services, a rabbi with specialized background in work with the mentally ill joined the staff. He expanded these religious services to other units in the Center, each unit developing its individual pattern depending on the group's membership. For example, he expanded the Friday afternoon service on the all-female unit by recreating the religious atmosphere of the traditional Jewish home with the Sabbath symbols of the white table cloth, the Sabbath menorah, wine and challah (braided white loaf of bread) set on the table at which the Jewish mother blessed the candles. The rabbi's presence gave these women much emotional sustenance, uplifting their mood. When the men were identified with the spiritual leader, I was able to withdraw. For seven years these religious services have continued on all the units of the very ill residents. The social service staff is no longer active in the program but the rabbi now has an assistant.

Implications

It was obvious that a number of the patients developed more stature as human beings in their own eyes and in the reflection of those around them. Throughout life many individuals are said to be engaged in a quest for an identity. As O. Hobart Mowrer (1961) has stated: "Once more we are coming to perceive man as pre-eminently a social creature, whose greatest and most devastating anguish is experienced, not in physical pain or biological deprivation, but when he feels alienated, disgraced, debased as a person" (p. 84).

Participating in rituals that have endured over centuries should give individuals the feeling of being part of an immortal strain rather than a transient in life. Further, sharing with a group in the ritual or expressing religious feelings through others added dimensions to the individual's existence.

Having the service in the unit expanded that life space, adding function and meaning to the environment of the men. Also, viewing them in the roles assumed during a service gave staff members, other residents, and family a new perspective of these residents. Identity and changing life space may be areas worthwhile to pursue in depth in a future study.

The emotion experienced in this program is essential and universal regardless of denomination or religious tradition.

Margaret Isherwood (1971) states: "If the goal of all religion is the increase of spiritual *being* in ourselves, the way of spiritual *becoming* is fundamentally the same for the Catholic, Methodist, Quaker, Vendantist, Baptist, Buddhist, Moslem, Taoist, Bahaist or Hindu" (p. 125).

Although this program was in an Orthodox Jewish institution, I believe it could work in any institution, sectarian or governmental, wherever there is a group within the institution whose early life included religious observance.

Such a program does not require special staff, merely someone with conviction about the value of investing the time and energy required to develop such a service. Sue W. Spencer (1957) says that a social worker should have this quality: "One would expect that the social worker who through his own religion has a great source of faith, courage, and joy will be able to convey to others this sense of strength and confidence in meeting the problems of life..." (pp. 520-521).

We speak of treating the whole person, yet programs for the aged generally are often more concerned with the physical and social aspects of rehabilitation. We are missing an important link if as clinicians we do not make use of the inner spiritual and cultural resources of the aged in our institutions as part of rehabilitation. Then, we might be able to agree in essence with Rabbi Albert S. Goldstein (1967): "Let your sense of wonder and your faith, joy, hope and zest in living grow...and you will never grow old."

This experiment in bringing religious services to a unit in which a group of very debilitated men resided was an effort to renew practices familiar to these men from their past. As much individual participation as possible was encouraged to make it their own program. Although initiated by a member of the social service department, it was later transferred to the institution's new rabbi, who was experienced in work with the mentally ill. It has become an ongoing process on a number of the units where the most severely mentally and physically ill male and female residents live. Utilization of the cultural and religious practices of our residents as part of our rehabiliation program continues.

REFERENCES

Goldstein, A.S. *Temple tidings.* Brookline, Mass.: Temple Ohabie Shalom Bulletin. November 24, 1967.

Isherwood, M. *Searching for meaning (a religion of inner-growth for agnostics and believers).* Philadelphia: Macrae Smith Co., 1971.

Jackson, E.N. Grief and religion. In Feifel, Herman (Ed.), *The meaning of death.* New York: McGraw-Hill, 1959.

Mowrer, O.H. Psychiatry and religion. *Atlantic Monthly, 84,* July, 1961.

Spencer, S.W. Religious and spiritual values in social casework practice. *Social Casework.* 1957, *38,* 520-521.

Zborowski, M., & Herzog, E. *Life is with people; the Jewish little town of Eastern Europe.* New York: International Universities Press, 1952.

Chapter 26

A PROGRAM TO REDUCE SPIRITUAL DEPRIVATION IN THE NURSING HOME

VICKI A. ZOOT

In September of 1976, Niles Township Jewish Congregation of Skokie, Illinois, moved to "adopt" Skokie Valley Terrace Nursing Center, a nursing home that is one of nine in a for-profit chain. Skokie Valley Terrace has 113 beds, 50 percent of which are occupied by Jewish residents. At the time of the adoption, there were no religious services being held there except for weekly communion for the Catholic residents.

The program started by organizing weekly Sabbath services and special holiday celebrations. The Social Action Committee of the Congregation has provided the leadership along with several other groups in the synagogue. Several of the women from the temple sisterhood are volunteer visitors on a weekly basis, others have donated ritual objects and flowers. One sisterhood member embroidered a challah cover. The Men's Club and the Social Action Committee have assumed the responsibility for special holiday celebrations and observances. The children of the religious school made gifts for the residents for Chanukah, and they came dressed in Purim costumes to deliver Shalach Monos. The residents hosted them to a party consisting of lemonade and hamentaschen, which the residents made under volunteer supervision.

The potential for the growth of this program is unlimited. Planned activities include expanding a curriculum on aging for the children in the religious school, a "rap" session on attitudes about aging, retirement planning for the adults, weekly intergenerational Bible classes at the home, and an oral history project connected to a family "Adopt-A-Grandparent" Program.

The residents at Skokie Valley Terrace Nursing Center are giving evidence that they are aware that the congregation at Niles

195

Township Jewish Congregation knows they are alive and care about them not only as fellow Jews but also as individuals who are worth caring about. They are becoming part of a congregation. The services give them an opportunity to be together in a community of friendship; their non-Jewish coresidents frequently attend services as their guests. the involvement with the synagogue gives them the opportunity to reverse the guest-host relationship; temple members are the guests in their home.

Observers of the program's success do not believe that all of the attendance is necessarily prompted by religious motivation. It may very well be that the socialization need that is met is responsible for the very large attendance. A religious program such as this can become the pivot for many therapeutically effective efforts.

Examples of the involvement of the adoption program include the Reality Orientation Services, which are held at the same time every week. The weekly Torah readings and candle lighting times both follow the same schedule. By observing holidays, there is always something to look forward to, to plan for, thus helping residents organize their time. Appropriate prayers are said for the dead and for those residents who are hospitalized. Using Jewish calendars, it is possible for the residents to remember their dead by observing yartzeits. They talk about the deceased and about missing them, thus accomplishing needed grief work. There is something about prayers that revives even the most deteriorated, nonfunctional resident. People whom the staff regards as vegetative are able to demonstrate a competency, and often start a stream of reminiscing. Very often services end, and a group of residents "hang around" and talk about the past; they have a very interested new audience and are able to do life reviewing. Several relatives of the residents have started to join their loved ones for services. The residents have taken on an importantly active role in setting up and participating in all of the activities. There are appropriate jobs for the incapacitated (passing out head covers is an ideal job for a wheelchair-bound resident stationed in the doorway of the room). The honors of lighting the candles, saying the Kadish, and the Hamotze are rotated among the residents. The residents help to plan and prepare for the holidays; they decide, often in a heated discussion, where to donate their Tzedakah money. Some seem to be paying more attention to their attire and their personal hygiene. The nursing home has accepted some of the responsibility for this involvement. The administrator provides the wine and pays for the challah. His staff, under the guidance of the activity director, sees to it that the residents are at the services, and the activity director publicizes special events and makes whatever arrangements are necessary for special programs. Observers have perceived an increase in morale of the nursing staff as a result of the community's involvement. Because of the participation of the volunteers, there has been a positive influence on the quality of the care provided in the home.

What Can You Do?

Persons involved in congregations might wish to ask themselves a number of questions:
1. Have we attempted to meet the needs of the elderly in our community?
2. Do we know where the housebound isolated elderly and chronically ill community members are located?
3. Do we know how many nursing homes there are in our area, and have we inquired as to whether or not they have religious services?
4. Are we really doing all we can?

Religious congregations and communities can be effective in bringing about positive change in long-term care. They can improve the quality of life for the aged and chronically ill institutionalized residents, and at the same time can improve the quality of life of the religious institutions themselves. Efforts such as these can be a revitalizing force in which the community, led by the religious institutions, can begin to see itself in a role in which it is critically needed.

Section VI
PUTTING SPIRITUAL WELL-BEING INTO PERSPECTIVE

Chapter 27

SPIRITUAL WELL-BEING AS A CELEBRATION OF WHOLENESS

Margaret S. Kuhn

As we explore what it means to become old and to be old in our society, we come into full understanding of life itself. Simone de Beauvoir in *The Coming of Age* (1972) states that the lack of meaning of age in any society puts that whole society to the test. The ethical possibilities of life are broader than any philosopher has guessed and stronger than any psychologist has suspected. Churches and synagogues today are called by our Creator, and by the tragic situation of our divided sick and ailing society, to be healers and liberators of the sick and the oppressed. Our society is being sorely tested about our present notion about age and by the blasphemous hypocrisy with which most approach age.

There is a great pervasive paternalism that accompanies our society's reponse to the fact of age. It is assumed by very well-meaning and dedicated people that somehow in the upper age brackets we enter a second childhood when we become not mature, responsible elders of the tribe but wrinkled babies. Much of what is done for us and to us, instead of with us, hastens the onslaught of wrinkled babyhood. If the church and synagogue are to meet the test of this society, their goal should be the encouragement of the large numbers of older people in congregations across the country toward mature, responsible adulthood.

Churches and synagogues are going to have to be engaged in a mighty ethical and moral confrontation with the prevailing values of our society. A holy war has to be waged by religious communities of the world, the communities of faith, to challenge and change the prevailing values of the postindustrial technological era that has put the bottom line always before people. Age challenges the church in many ways. The challenge to the church

and the synagogue is to forget and put aside all forms of paternalism and to monitor each other when it creeps into our
language, into our policy, and into our behavior. Billions of tax
dollars from the states and from federal funding are going into
maintaining a pervasive paternalism that is destructive and from
which we must be free. In order for the church and the synagogue
to have any real credibility, they must change the order of things.

Every piece of age-segregated housing that is being developed
under religious auspices should be stopped. The plans should be
torn up, thrown away, burned. In every age-segregated housing
facility, there ought to be child care centers, there ought to be
nursery schools, there ought to be tutoring arrangements with the
very young. Only by such extraordinary means can we correct the
oppression that we have created by the idea that older people like
to live by themselves. Vacant college dormitories ought to be used
by old people, and there ought to be cross-generational living and
learning going on all over the country by putting the old and the
young together. This would bridge the gap, the horrible separation of the two, that has been so destructive for both groups.

Celebration means that we have a new opportunity in our
times to refresh our minds. One of the mythologies about old age
that we have been persuaded to believe is that old people cannot
learn; somehow after age fifty or fifty-five our brain grows soft,
and it is just a question of time before senility begins. There have
been some very substantial research studies that show that indeed
there is no real loss of reflective cognitive power in old age.
Religious institutions that are concerned about education and
the nurture of the mind should lead society in the encouragement
of the older people in congregations to go back to school, to learn.

The religious congregation and the community of faith have
an ongoing task that must be seen in a new way. The proclamation of the word could emphasize the concept that there are in old
age the opportunities for the elders of the congregation to share.
The preaching of the word could include the very vigorous
experiences of old people who have known oppression and who
have lived through it in their lives. Examples are found in the
marvelous memories and the keen sense of injustice of elderly
Jews in this country. These people are alive and constitute a very

precious human resource, but most of them are not in the position to be that kind of resource. For one thing, we consider them a drag. For another, we have deprived them through retirement laws of any kind of useful place in society. These people have something to give us; they represent a very powerful, motivating force that we have overlooked. Through the proclamation of the word from our pulpits, those people can tell how it is and how it was. They can give us a vision of how it ought to be in the future.

Pastoral counseling is a traditional and wonderful function, but there are dimensions of pastoral counseling that have yet to be explored. For example, the dimensions of human sexuality take on a new meaning and a new sensitivity in old age. One of the myths is that old age is sexless, and that we have lost in our old age the capacity or the need to love and be loved or to express any kind of sexual response. That is a cruel conditioning that deprives us of the ground of our being. There are no more appropriate counselors than people in the churches and synagogues, who could help people get hold of their human sexuality to cherish it and affirm it in loving, wise, and appropriate ways.

There are all kinds of dimensions in human relations, in marital relations, that counselors in the churches and the synagogues have to get into. Not every grieving, lonely widow ought to be permitted to live alone in a big old house. There ought to be some kind of communal-cooperative lifestyle, shared use of space, or shared use of human resources. Many of us in our later years cannot live alone and really live well, comfortably, safely. We need each other. We have competed too long. In our old age it is appropriate for us to demonstrate how to cooperate, how to live together in true human communities. Congregations could be in essence and in reality extended families, reconstituting the clan family, which we have largely forsaken and destroyed. Congregations could be those families, supportive, loving communities, that enable the members to live well together. Churches and synagogues should encourage and bless those kinds of opportunities.

The churches and synagogues are called upon to be a very wise and discerning critic and judge of our society. Much of our society is sick, some of it is dying, and some of it is dead. The welfare system is sick. The health system is not health care but sickness care. The emphasis ought to be on self-help and self-healing, through the reality of the supportive community that can love and forgive and help to heal its members. That is one of the great challenges of congregational life today. As the religious community attempts to heal itself and to deal with its own life in a new way, it has a very important message and judgment to convey to the secular society. As we are talking about health, we cannot skip over the abuses and the tragedy of institutional care, particularly nursing homes. There ought to be a holy war waged against the kind of malpractice, neglect, and cruel oppression that have been a part of that horrible scene.

Finally, the church has a great and glorious opportunity to affirm the ethical, biblical, and theological base for us to do what we must do in the world. Without some mature, secure understanding of who we are and what our faith instructs us to do, we are not going to be able to challenge the value system of our society. Without this, we are not going to be able to engage the demonic forces that make our society so sick. The seminaries with some rare exceptions are grossly neglecting the largest, most rapidly growing segment of our American society. It is up to the congregations and the people to see that this gross neglect is corrected. In our time, the strength of old people could be affirmed and seen in a new light. Seldom do the churches and synagogues celebrate our strength. It must be providential, in God's plan, that there are so many of us, close to 23 million sixty-five years and older. It may be that God looked down upon our sick and ailing and divided world and said, "Aha! I will raise some new revolutionaries to point the way." It might be that those of us who are nearest death could be chosen by God to point to where new life can be found.

REFERENCE

de Beauvoir, Simone. *The coming of age.* New York: Putnam's Sons, 1972.

A CASE STUDY OF SPIRITUAL WELL-BEING
John W. Stettner

The National Interfaith Coalition on Aging's definition of spiritual well-being is: "Spiritual well-being is the affirmation of life in a relationship with God, self, community and environment that nurtures and celebrates wholeness." When I first saw this definition and its accompanying commentary about two years ago, I was immediately impressed with it. Subsequently, as I reflected upon it, I began to wonder what spiritual well-being, so defined, might look like in a real live person. I was interested in thinking about how a person achieves spiritual well-being, why some people seem to have it and others do not. I was already assuming that it is not simply a matter of choice, the result of the "power of positive thinking." Neither could I believe that it is inherent, something that some people are simply born with and others are not. On the other hand, I do not believe that an arbitrary God bestows spiritual well-being on some and not on others. My speculation was, and is, that all three of these elements, as well as others, probably have some part to play in any given instance of spiritual well-being. In other words, my working assumption is that a person is born with unknown potential capacities; the physical and interpersonal environment have much to do with how those capacities develop; as the person grows and develops, he has more possibility of choices, which then affect his future development; and finally, I have a sense that the will of the Creator-God is somehow working itself out in the lives of persons. As I thought about all this, a man I know came to mind, because he seems to me to be a living example of the NICA definition more so than anyone else of whom I can think. I decided to check out my hunch and interview the gentleman. I did not initially show him the NICA definition or tell him what I was thinking. I simply told him that I would like to talk with him about his life story and particularly about his religious faith.

205

My subject is an eighty-year-old white male, a retired minister. He was born, the seventh of eight children, in a small town in Indiana, into a family having German and English forebears. His father was a glass-blower and farmer. The family never had much money, but they were not victimized by severe poverty either. Our subject, N, is the only member of his family to go to college. N had a normal childhood, attending the local elementary and high schools. He was rather an average student but was always very interested and involved in sports. N's parents were not members of, and never attended, church. Near the family home was a Christian (Disciples of Christ) Church, and N and some of his siblings went to Sunday School and worship at this church. One of N's vivid memories from childhood is the idea of the Devil that was common in the community, especially among the church people. The Devil was described in detail: a grotesque figure in a red suit, with horns and a tail. N remembers an evening when he was with some older children, including one or two of his brothers, when they were talking about the Devil, and N felt that he could actually see this horrible figure. He ran home and went to bed, crying himself to sleep, but never telling anyone about his experience. Some time after this experience N and a friend attended a revival meeting at the church and they both responded to an "altar call," to come forward and declare their faith in Jesus Christ. Subsequently N was baptized by the pastor of the church in a stream at the edge of town, as church members stood by singing hymns. No member of his family was present on this occasion, but N remembers driving the horse and wagon home feeling very good about the experience.

The church people made N feel very welcome and accepted. Some of the men urged him to go to Transylvania College in Kentucky, a school that was affiliated with the Christian Church. N had no money, but by working and receiving a little scholarship help he was able to make it. He spent four happy years at Transylvania, in the course of which he had the opportunity to hear persons like Robert Speer and John R. Mott, who came to the college to speak. Though it was a church-related college, N recalls that several of his professors were great liberals in terms of their social concern and their theological orientation. One of these professors recommended N for a Y.M.C.A. scholarship following his graduation. He received the scholarship for graduate study at Columbia University, and so N went to New York City. The scholarship was negligible, and so N took a job as a youth worker in a church that was in the section of New York known as "Hell's Kitchen." After a while he was ordained as a minister in the Christian Church, which did not require a seminary degree. Meanwhile, however, N did begin to take some courses at Union Seminary.

One of the outstanding experiences for N at Union was the course he had under Harry Emerson Fosdick, entitled the "Modern Use of the Bible." N says of Fosdick, "He took down one pillar of faith but put two back." N commented that he was able to leave his conservative background without losing faith. When asked how he thought he had been able to accomplish this, he replied that it just seemed to be his "nature" not to be afraid to leave tradition and try new things. In this connection, he observed that his father always farmed in old-fashioned, traditional ways, whereas N felt that if he had been a farmer he would have tried to utilize the latest scientific methods in his work. In any event, the liberal atmosphere around Union and Columbia, exemplified by Fosdick and others, was very congenial to N; he was inspired and enlivened by it.

A Presbyterian minister whom N knew in New York City became pastor of a large church in upstate New York and invited N to join him as an associate. While there, N transferred into the Presbyterian denomination. He subsequently served as an associate minister in two other large, urban Presbyterian churches, retiring at about seventy years of age. The major emphases in his ministry were Christian education and pastoral work, especially the latter.

While he was in New York City, N met a midwestern girl who was doing graduate work at Teacher's College, Columbia. Later, when he was at the church in upstate New York, they were married. They subsequently had four children. The family has always been, and is, close-knit. Looking back on the years when the children were growing up, N commented that he thinks some women would not have tolerated his behavior, because he spent so much time on his ministerial work. He expressed some regret that he had not given more time to his family and had not done more reading and study. However, he immediately gave his reason for doing as he did — where there was human need he always felt obliged to do something about it, and of course, there are always many needs. With a minimum of complaining, his wife and children endured, and the retirement years for N and his wife have been extremely happy ones.

N declares that he and his family have been "fortunate" since they have never had any serious illnesses, deaths, or other tragedies in their immediate family with which to cope. One of the children made an unhappy marriage and was divorced but is now happily remarried. N notes that they have all had their ups and downs, but all in the normal course of events. He often expresses gratitude for the goodness of their family's life and is highly motivated to share his good fortune with others. Thus, in his retirement years, N has been constantly busy performing pastoral and other kinds of tasks on a volunteer basis in the community. He and his wife have led numerous tours to all parts of the world, and their interest in the places they have visited is always much deeper than the typical sight-seeing level of the tourist. Indeed, wherever possible, N has tried to observe and visit with some common people in the countries they have visited. He and his wife can give fascinating reports, with pictures, of their trips.

N has always been interested in and loved nature. He was a pioneer in the idea of church camping programs, and part of his concern in this regard was to help persons (especially children) become more alive to the beauty and wonder of God's creation. He has for many years had large gardens every summer, growing both flowers and vegetables. He is an avid bird watcher and builder of bird houses. He is interested in ecology and tries in whatever ways he can to promote a healthy balance in the natural world around him. He frequently executes or spearheads ecological projects in the community where he lives.

One of the most characteristic things about N is his interest in and concern for other people. Living in a retirement complex himself, he seeks constantly to minister to his fellow residents as well as persons in other similar facilities in the community. For a time he gave volunteer service to a nursery school, helping young children learn how to handle some simple tools. N is not very partisan in his political views, but he is interested in current issues. Also, on any election day he is likely to be busy driving persons to polling places so they can vote. In the course of his long ministry and life, N has seen almost every conceivable kind of human suffering and wickedness. However, he never seems to give up on anyone; any situation, no matter how bad, can always be made a little bit better. For untold numbers of people he has turned up at exactly the right moment with a saving word of hope or comfort.

Another outstanding characteristic of N is his relationship with God. He maintains regular Bible study and prayer, and he seems in a very real way to "practice the presence of God." Indeed, listening to and observing N from this perspective, what comes to mind are the words of the Latvian folk song:

> My God and I walk through the fields together,
> We walk and talk as good friends should and do....

N is a friend of God, in the sense in which the patriarchs of the Bible were God's friends. Thus God is not a soft-hearted pal to be manipulated, nor someone who is so familiar as to run the danger of becoming contemptible, nor yet a being so tender that He cannot be argued with nor be the occasional object of anger. The essential characteristic seems to be closeness, with a sense of profound respect.

I do not wish to portray N as a superhuman paragon of virtue, righteousness, and holiness, yet all that I have said about him is true and much more could be said. Everyone, however, is not always so positively impressed or affected by him. He is very "human," as we say, and he would be the first to admit it. As an example of a person who "affirms life, in a relationship with God, self, community and environment, that nurtures and celebrates wholeness," I think N is an example par excellence. He certainly affirms life, busy as he is each day, and is always looking forward to tomorrow. He is certainly on good terms with himself, has deep concerns for the environment, is widely involved in the community, and has a beautiful relationship with God.

However, this is only one type of human experience. Not everyone's life story is so happy, nor could their sense of spiritual well-being be described in these terms. The NICA definition of spiritual well-being is well illustrated by a case like N, but could it be stretched to cover other types of experience? Reflecting on this, it occurred to me that the language of the definition is very reminiscent of what William James (1929) described as the "healthy-minded type."

The Varieties of Religious Experience is the book that resulted from the Gifford Lectures that James delivered at Edinburgh in 1902. It is a classic in the field of the psychology of religion. In one of his lectures James called attention to "The enormous diversities which the spiritual lives of different men exhibit. Their wants their susceptibilities, and their capacities all vary and must be classed under different heads. The result is that we have really different types of religion experience" (p. 107). James's basic typology is a simple one, consisting of the "healthy-minded" and the "sick soul." He quotes Francis W. Newman, who delineated "the once-born and the twice-born" as the two families of children God has on this earth (p. 79). It is the "once-born" that correspond to James' "healthy-minded" type. The "twice-born" corresponds to James' "sick soul." We must not, however, be misled by the popular, common sense connotations of the terms "healthy-minded" and "sick soul," for there is no implied valuation in James's use of the terms. In fact, he suggests that it is the "sick soul" that probably has the more profound understanding of life. The point is, though, that the "once-born" or "healthy-minded" type of person has a religious experience just as valid as the other type. It is to this "healthy-minded" type that we are giving our major attention in this chapter.

James defines the healthy-minded type as:

> The temperament which has a constitutional incapacity for prolonged suffering, and in which the tendency to see things optimistically is like a water of crystallization in which the individual's character is set.... This temperament may become the basis for a (particular) type of religion, a

religion in which good, even the good of this world's life, is regarded as the essential thing for a rational being to attend to. (p. 125)

Elsewhere James puts the matter is less formal terms: "There are men who seem to have started in life with a bottle or two of champagne inscribed to their credit; whilst others seem to have been born close to the pain-threshold, which the slightest irritants fatally send them over" (p. 133).

Let us be clear that we are talking about basic personality types that by and large do not change over a lifetime, and not simply passing moods. James is pointing to a characteristic way of perceiving life and acting accordingly. Even the healthy-minded person has low moments when things are not as good as they might be; even the "sick soul" has moments when things seem unaccountably good. As James says, "Every abstract way of conceiving things selects some one aspect of them as their essence for the time being, and disregards the other aspects" (p. 86). A little further on he says, "When happiness is actually in possession, the thought of evil can no more acquire the feeling of reality than the thought of good can gain reality when melancholy rules" (p. 87).

I am suggesting that the implication for us is that the NICA definition of spiritual well-being, and our case study illustrating it, constitute one valid understanding of human experience. There is at least one other type of perspective on the meaning of spiritual well-being, though, and that type corresponds to the "sick soul" in William James's typology. James, of course, does not speak directly to the issue of spiritual well-being in regard to either of his types, but to describe the perspective of the "sick soul," he says:

Not the conception or intellectual perception of evil, but the grizzly blood-freezing heart-palsying sensation of it close upon one, and no other conception or sensation is able to live for a moment in its presence. How irrelevantly remote seem all our usual refined optimisms and intellectual and moral consolations in presences of a need of help like this! Here is the real core of the religious problem: Help! Help! No prophet can claim to bring a final message unless he says things that will have a sound of reality in the ears of victims such as these. (p. 159)

This description obviously fits a quite different type of experience than that dealt with in the NICA definition of spiritual well-being.

It would be interesting to reflect on what might be described as spiritual well-being for one of James's sick souls. It is not assumed that the sick souls, in James's definition, are the pathological exceptions to the majority rule, there are plenty of them around, and some of them must have achieved a state that could be called "spiritual well-being." How could it be defined with such a person, and what would a living example look like? Some of James's concluding comments about the sick soul provide a clue:

> It seems to me that we are bound to say that morbid-mindedness (the sick soul) ranges over the wider scale of experience, and that its survey is the one that overlaps. The method of averting one's attention from evil, and living simply in the light of the good is splendid as long as it will work. It will work with many persons; it will work for more generally than most of us are ready to suppose; and within the sphere of its successful operation there is nothing to be said against it as a religious solution. But it breaks down impotently as soon as melancholy comes; and even though one be quite free from melancholy oneself, there is no doubt that healthy-mindedness is inadequate as a philosophical doctrine, because the evil facts which it refuses positively to account for are a genuine portion of reality; and they may after all be the best key to life's significance, and possibly the only openers of our eyes to the deepest levels of truth.
>
> The normal process of life contains moments as bad as any of those which insane (pathological) melancholy is filled with, moments in which radical evil gets its innings and takes its solid turn. (p. 160)

The task remains to try to describe and illustrate what "spiritual well-being" might mean with a "sick soul" whose religious experience is of the "twice-born" variety. I am convinced that such a task could be done, and one would not have to look very far in the Bible and great devotional literature to get some clues, nor should finding an example to write up as a case study be difficult either.

I will conclude with an observation or two about the nature of the relevance of the NICA definition. This description of spiritual well-being, and the kind of experience it represents, accords well with the positive, optimistic American dream, which is still thriving. Also, it is probably part of a larger movement of thought that is current in many places around the earth—a movement that might be briefly but inadequately described as humanistic. During the last century mankind has witnessed some of the most awful examples of man's inhumanity to man in all human history, so there is presently a reaction to this in attempting to accentuate the positive and reinforce the best in human nature. Who can quarrel with that? Spiritual well-being, whatever that may mean, is a goal to be strived for by young and old, by the "healthy-minded" and the "sick soul." Assuredly, the sick souls may achieve something that could be called spiritual well-being, though they would probably describe it in terms quite different from the NICA definition. One brief example is a quotation from that great giant of the faith, Martin Luther, as quoted by William James: "I am utterly weary of life. I pray the Lord will come forthwith and carry me hence. Let him come, above all, with his last Judgment; I will stretch out my neck, the thunder will burst forth, and I shall be at rest" (p. 135).

Thus, we must tune our ears to quite differently worded messages that may in their own ways convey a sense of spiritual well-being. Finally, for all the effort that is appropriately expended to help persons achieve *psychological* health (that is, a way of coping with life, having some self-esteem and decent relations with the community and environment), let us not forget that it is God who gives his faithful creatures a sense of *spiritual* well-being.

REFERENCES

James, W. *The varieties of religious experience.* New York: Longmans, Green, & Co., 1929.

Chapter 29

SPIRITUAL AND RELIGIOUS DIMENSIONS OF AGING: APPLICATIONS

ELBERT COLE

An examination of some of the spiritual and religious dimensions of aging helps to provide an understanding of the nature of the specialized job that the church and people of faith bring the whole theme of aging. Our fundamental task is to really understand the rich diversity of older people themselves. We often, even those of us who indicate that we are interested in working with older people, give indications that we think monolithically, we think of older people as being all alike: if you've seen one, you've seen all of them. Older people appreciate those working with them who have some understanding of the total diversity and richness of their lives.

There comes a time when people reach that magic age and begin to act like what they assume one is supposed to act like when they are no longer in the production system. No longer drawing their sense of purpose and meaning from their work and their task, they then move into a kind of wilderness; they are really looking for liberation. They are dealing with how they can handle the finiteness of their life with erosions and various limitations that begin to impinge upon them.

The question that older people are asking more than any other question is, "What is the meaning and purpose of life? What's it all about?" This is a religious question. Obviously, it is the age-old question that the church has tried to deal with with all people. What does it all add up to? We sometimes forget that many people have found their sense of identity, their sense of well-being, largely from the kind of work they do. We forget how indelibly this has been etched into our mind-set, into our thinking. Who then are you, as a person who once was? Who are

214

you now? How do you identify? How do you capture some sense of identity?

How, within the spiritual and religious dimension, in the field of aging, can we deal with what presents itself as one of the urgent needs of people: needing to know how they can continue to be useful? How can we translate that? Of course, there are the stories of Grandma Moses and all of the artists and the musicians and the statesmen who make rich contributions in late life to our society—we know all of that. The real question is: how do you translate that to the people in your block, the ordinary kind of people? How can they indicate in society that they are making some contribution to life? One way that we begin to understand the religious and spiritual dimension of our existence is to begin to help people make this role change. The religious and spiritual sector needs to give attention to providing an arena where people can handle this kind of gnawing anxiety about life and its purpose and its nature. The church has not really dealt with the issue of helping people to deal with the issues of the later years, particularly in seeing them in new dimensions. The church has to press itself to deal with the whole question of the meaning of life and the passages of life. This requires an intentional ministry. This kind of ministry just does not happen. One of the dilemmas in this area is: How do you break all of the stereotypes and restraints that are possessed by the people who are supposed to be the dreamers? How do you break them so that they, in turn, can then train others? Too many pastors imagine their own ministry in the classical, traditional forms of one-to-one ministry, sort of a pastoral ministry, or they think of it as a ministry to that small portion of society in need of institutional care.

The Christian heresy is the heresy of dividing life into things physical and things spiritual. We have to mend that constantly in helping people see the unity of the total being. Religious questions for older people begin at the point of their very existence—what holds the whole life together. That pushes us in the end to shoring up people with what might be called social services in order for people to be able to survive. More directly, older people are asking basic questions dealing with the anxieties of life, which are religious questions.

The whole question of usefulness, the sense of participation in the family of life and of man, is a religious question. Who needs me? The religious and spiritual sectors of our community need to be awakened, to be challenged, that the fundamental task in our society is not in the political sector; the fundamental task is a religious question. The fundamental task of aging in our time is the meaning question. It is to help a society chart the wilderness, become liberated in these years, to move into the pool of Bethesda, to discover the finite and infinite dimensions of our existence. We really need to engage ourselves in enabling people to discover the purpose and the meaning of their life. We are still too close to it to do more than to provide models, to continue research, to bring to bear all that we possibly can in a kind of a haphazard, scattered way. However, we recognize that it is a task that needs to be performed.

The church is heavily engaged right now in imitating the political sector. Local congregations rush out to simply duplicate what government programs and various agencies are suggesting ought to be done. The real task is to go back to the people to discover again what people really need in their lives and how they can be shored up, how they can be brought through the rough places. That takes social services, specific kinds of the various social services that need to be done. We need to design an intentional ministry for older people.

All that we say about intentional ministry in congregational life needs to be applied now to this age bracket. What are the specific functions that the church must perform? As we begin to discover some of the answers, we are also sensitive to some of the obstacles. An example is the recognition that the word "old" is a word that conjures up disease, unworthiness, unimportance, insignificance. We must recognize that society is dominated by disease concepts of aging. Then we must begin to introduce into the life of congregations such exciting things as adventures, creativeness, new problem solving, new ways to reaffirm life, celebrations of values to affirm for a younger generation what an older generation has discovered to be worthwhile. This will help us to discover again something of the pricelessness of life itself and to appraise the fact that the tragedy is not that people die, but that people never live. A church that does not reach its youth is one generation away from extinction, but a church that does not really reach and deal meaningfully with its adults is already dead.

The result of our work in Kansas City is not the work that a minister does—it is simply enabling older people themselves to be caught up in a whole series of systems by which life can be supported and people can survive. Through the efforts of older people a meaning and purpose can be discovered. This does not become another heavy program that is laid on the parish minister, but rather it becomes an integral part of congregational life. It can redeem a congregation and cause a congregation to realize that we are dealing with the ultimate religious question— the question of our existence and the question of what it means to be a person in the larger family of man.

Chapter 30

RELIGIOUS LIFE OF THE ELDERLY: MYTH OR REALITY?

BARBARA PITTARD PAYNE

R eligion is generally assumed to become increasingly important in old age and older people are considered to be
more religious than younger persons. These religious stereotypes
are explained by yet another stereotype; older people become
more religious because they are anticipating their own death, or,
as the flippant explanation goes, older people are more religious
because they are cramming for finals. Yet, research to support
these assumptions about the importance of religion and religious
institutions in the lives of older people is limited and frequently
contradictory. The historical basis for the research contradiction
can be traced to Starbuck, the pioneer of the psychology of
religion who, in 1911, reported that religious faith and belief in
God grow in importance as the years advance (his aging category
was forty and over) and to another psychologist, Stanley Hall
who, in 1922, found that older people became no more religious
as they age. Gerontologists and social scientists have neglected
this area of research to the extent that Edward Heenan (1968) calls
religion and aging, at least for sociologists, the empirical
lacunae. Such neglect suggests that gerontologists do not consider
religion and religious institutions significant dimensions in
aging or as sources of social support for the elderly. Thus, we are
faced with the question: Are these stereotypes or assumptions
about religious life of the elderly myth or reality?

The purpose of this chapter is to attempt to resolve this issue
by: (1) summarizing what we know about the religious life of the
elderly from the research literature, from our own participation,
observation, and interviews with 325 older volunteers, and from a
national study of religious commitment (N=208); (2) examining

218

the treatment of religion and aging in major works in geronto-logy; (3) examining the inclusion of papers or sections on religion in the gerontology professional meetings; and (4) examining some research and policy recommendations.

What do we know about the religious beliefs, attitudes, and practices of the elderly? Most of what we know is based on a limited number of empirical studies and most of these are ten to twenty-five years old:

1.   Ninety-seven percent of the elderly claim they have a religious preference (U.S. Bureau of the Census, 1958).
2.   Older people are more likely to be church members than members of any other one type of voluntary association (Payne, Payne and Reddy, 1972).
3.   Attendance at a church or religious service is slightly higher for people over sixty-five years of age but becomes less regular in advanced old age (Wingrove and Alston, 1971). However, Orback (1961) found that age per se was unrelated to changes in church attendance.
4.   Attendance at religious services does not increase signi-ficantly with age, but the importance that people attach to religion in their lives does (Harris, 1975; Cavan, Burgess, Havighurst, and Goldhamer, 1949; Payne 1977).
5.   Attendance at religious services shows little decline until the seventies; this usually is a consequence of a health change or change in family composition (Riley and Foner, 1968; Lowenthal and Robinson, 1976).
6.   The elderly spend more time in private religious practice, such as Bible reading, prayer, or listening to or viewing religious programs, than younger people or than they did at a younger age (Moberg, 1970).
7.   The amount of time spent in the devotional, at home religious activities increases when church attendance de-clines (Moberg, 1975; Stark, 1968).
8.   Women are more active in church activities than older men (Albrecht, 1958; Bahr, 1970).
9.   Regular attendance at church services declines less for women aged seventy-five and over than it does for men

(Taietz and Larson, 1956; Cumming and Henry, 1961; Orback, 1961; Dumazedier, 1974).

10. Religious conviction becomes more salient over the years for those who already believe (Moberg, 1968; Payne, 1965).

11. Older people tend to adhere to more orthodox or conservative religious viewpoints than younger people (Moberg, 1968; Schuyler, 1959; Fukuyoma, 1961).

12. Older people are more likely to believe in immortality (life after death) than younger people (Moberg, 1970).

13. Religion and religious activity are related to the elderly's concept of death. Positive or forward-looking death attitudes are held by actively religious elderly (Swenson, 1961; Feifel, 1964; Stark, 1968). Older believers (whether religious or atheist) have fewer death fears compared to older people who are uncertain (Kalish, 1976).

14. Religious study courses attract more people in their fifties and beyond more regularly than any other form of adult education (Moberg, 1968; Payne, 1973).

15. Happiness and religiosity are related for older people (O'Reilly, 1957; Palmore, 1969; Blazer and Palmore, 1976).

16. The correlation between religion and a more abundant sense of life satisfaction is not clear, but, with caution, the evidence seems to be in favor of this correlation (Moberg, 1968).

In addition to the contradictions in the research data, the methodology used (most are cross-sectional studies), the limited samples, the types of measures used, and the age of many of the studies make generalizations hazardous. The problem, as Moberg has suggested (1968), may be more in the concept "religion" than in the paucity of research. Furthermore, most of the measures of religion are crude and frequently added on to a research project with little attention paid to their validity and reliability or to the period bias of the items. We should be cautious about relying on the existing data for more than the beginning point of research in the years to come. Nevertheless, we do have enough evidence to assert that religion, private and institutional, persists in the form of significant and meaningful activities, beliefs, and roles into late life. What we do not know is in what ways religious behavior is practiced, modified, or meaningful.

Other observations support this conclusion. The elderly in preparation for and at the 1971 White House Conference on Aging identified spiritual needs as one of the seven major concerns of older persons and made specific recommendations about what the government and religious institutions should and could do to meet these needs. However, neither governmental agencies nor gerontologists and social scientists have responded. In a review of governmentally funded research in aging for the past ten years, we identified only one study that was specifically designed to study religion or the religiosity of the aged (Cook, 1976). Other studies of aging may have included a religious section or variable, but in only one was religion the primary concern of the researchers. Perhaps governmental funding agencies are acting on the national policy of separation of church and state, and the professional organizations have been influenced and operated on a policy of the separation of science and religion. Whatever the basic policy, the fact remains that from 1920 to 1970 there are few research studies on religion and aging, and there have been even fewer since the 1971 White House Conference.

An examination of the program abstracts of the Gerontological Society's Annual Scientific Meeting since 1963 yielded only six papers related to religion and aging and one of these was not based on research. Three of these were included in one session in the 1975 meetings—the only incidence found of a semi-sectional emphasis on religion.

Our next question is: How is religion treated in major works on aging? A number of recent books on aging were reviewed. The latest and most significant is the *Handbook on Aging and the Social Sciences* (Binstock and Shanas, 1976). It devotes approximately three columns to religion and these are within three chapters: one and one-half columns on aging and non-industrial societies (Goody, 1976), one column on social networks and isolation (Lowenthal and Robinson, 1976), and a half column on death in a social context (Kalish, 1976). This is not in proportion to the attention devoted to religious roles in the Riley and Foner

(1968) inventory of research findings and represents a dramatic change from a section fifty-one pages in length in the earlier *Handbook of Social Gerontology* (Tibbitts, 1960). Compared to the 1960 *Handbook* and the honored position that Maves's (1960) chapter has had in gerontological literature, we wonder what criteria were used by the editors of the more recent work to omit even a minor intentional treatment of religion and aging.

In terms of the content of the limited treatment of religion in the 1976 *Handbook*, Jack Goody devotes one and one-half columns to religious roles in non-industrial societies. His major point is that while elderly kings or tribal leaders are likely to be moved out of the political system, elderly priests move into dominant positions in the religious sphere. The dominance of elders in religious roles is accounted for by their assumed accumulation of knowledge and their proximity to the ancestors. With one foot in the grave they are the most likely intermediaries with the gods and the ancestors; their physical weakness makes their curses and blessings more powerful (Goody, 1976). Marjorie Fiske Lowenthal and Betsy Robinson (1976) subsume religion under a section on voluntary associations and their relationship to social networks and isolation. Church membership by the elderly is presented as an exception to the generalization from the research cited by Riley and Foner (1968) that the majority of older people do not belong to voluntary associations. Even with the church membership exception, they point out that membership per se tells us little and that participation in church-related groups declines with age. Thus, in half a paragraph, religion is dismissed as a significant social network or as having any important relationship to social isolation, unless it is to increase it.

Richard Kalish (1976) identifies religion as one of the major correlates of death fear. He finds a major source of confusion in the frequently simplistic measures that are used for operationalizing both religiousness and the fear of death. Kalish includes a condensed and succinct statement of the research on religiosity and death anxiety.

Riley and Foner's (1968) identification of research findings devotes an entire chapter to religious roles. They conclude that the data on religious roles, though substantial, contribute less on the whole than data on other roles, such as the political, to understanding aging as a process. However, they point out that evidence to support this conclusion comes almost entirely from cross-sectional studies, and that the samples are generally inadequate to support any full analysis of the complex factors apparently confounding the relationship between aging and religion. They do not conclude that for these reasons religious roles should not be investigated or are not significant. They call for longitudinal studies, better sampling methods, and suggest specific areas for investigation by social scientists in aging and religion.

Although Robert Butler and Myrna Lewis do not devote more than three pages to religion in *Aging and Mental Health* (1977), they indicate it is a significant role and social support for the elderly. They present religion as a solace to the frail and as filling a void for elderly women. They also cite the role of the clergy as counselors for the aged.

The Duke Longitudinal Studies, as reported in *Normal Aging I & II* (Palmore, 1970 and 1974), do not list religion in the index of Volume I but do include religion in the report on long-term adaptations by the elderly to bereavement, its relation to leisure activities, and understanding aging as a process. However, it is pointed out that evidence to support these relationships comes almost entirely from cross-sectional studies, and the samples are generally inadequate to support any full analysis of the complex factors apparently confounding the relationship between aging and religion. It is not concluded that for these reasons religious roles should not be studied or are not significant; rather, longitudinal studies and better sampling methods are called for, and specific areas for investigation by social scientists in aging and religion are suggested.

One paragraph and a quote from psychologist Stanley Hall (1922) constitutes the entire treatment of religion in Woodruff and Birren's *Aging* (1975). It would seem that Hall's conclusions in 1922 that "people did not necessarily show an increase in religion as they grow older nor do they become more fearful of death" satisfied their need in 1975 for investigation of this area of social behavior of the elderly.

Moberg's eleven page analytical review of religiosity research in the gerontological literature, done in 1965, is the only content on religion that Bernice Neugarten included in her social psychology reader, *Middle Age and Aging* (1968).

Kimmel (1974) devotes three pages to reporting on religion and church attendance, the importance of religion in late life, and the needs of the elderly. He attributes the change in church attendance in late life to the "increased interiority of the personality in that religion is more internal and less externally practiced in old age." However, Kimmel does point out that this may simply reflect that the aged have more chronic illnesses and are thus restricted in their ability to attend. Kimmel attributes the importance of religion in late life to the need for hope, meaning, and wholeness so that it is possible to accept one's own death, for "an old man who cannot bid farewell to life appears feeble and sickly as a young man who cannot embrace it."

A short but incisive section on religion is included in Hendricks and Hendricks's *Aging and Mass Society* (1977). They attempt very successfully to interpret the meaning of religion to the aged.

In contrast, we report from our participant observation reports the following incident as an indicant of the real meaning of religion to certain older people. In speaking to groups of older people in various sections of the United States, we invite them to write about what religion has meant to them throughout their lives—a kind of religious life review. Many of them take this as seriously as it is intended. A woman resident of a Colorado retirement village wrote:

> You asked about what religion has meant in our lives. I find I have to give you a resume of my relation to Christian work through the years. In 1920, my mother and I attended a mission conference at my home college. I refused to attend a mission talk with my mother, as they usually wanted nurses and I was not one. She woke me up at eleven that night and told me the first position was for a mathematics teacher for a girl's school in China. I know that I had no question and I am sure she had none that I was being pointed at. I applied and taught in China for four years, and I married an engineer that I met there. Since then there was never any question in my mind that doors would be opened for us if we had vision

enough to recognize them. When I came to Sunny Acres I supposed that much of my work through the years both with my own church and with the united work would stop. I served on the National Board of Church Women United from 1950-56 and so am familiar with other churches as well as my own. When I settled here the door of opportunity opened again and I found that I could still be of use. I am serving in both my church and also in the community United Church Women nearby. So far, the Lord has been good to me healthwise and incomewise. As I look back on our years I am more and more conscious of the hand of God working in our lives. So many times when things happen we do not realize that we are being directed. (Payne, 1977)

Research and Policy Recommendations

From this review of the research on aging and religion, the treatment of religion in the major gerontological publications, and the inclusion of papers and sections on religion at the Gerontological Society annual meetings, the following research and policy recommendations are suggested:

1. The positive and negative correlations of life satisfaction and religion may reflect the presence of other than religious factors. It is suggested that a more subtle use of statistical measures such as regression analysis might establish the salience of selected factors.
2. The definition of the concept of religion may account for the magnitude of the research problem as much as the paucity of data on religion and aging.
3. Measures of religiosity used in previous research should be evaluated in terms of their reliability and validity rather than using them without study.
4. There is a need for longitudinal studies to investigate the changes in the meaning of religion that seem to occur with aging.
5. Coordination and communication of research findings and methodology is needed through publication and presentation at national meetings.
6. Requests for more papers and sections on religion and aging in the various professional meetings, *e.g.*, The American Sociological Association, Society for the Scien-

tific Study of Religion, American Psychological Association, and The Gerontological Society should be made.
7. A greater effort should be made to develop more adequate measures of life satisfaction and religiosity.

Conclusion

The preceding review of research about the religious life of the elderly suggests several conclusions. First, it seems clear that there is both myth and reality about the importance to and practice of religion by the aged. The failure to relate health and age differences within the category sixty-five and over is the source of much of the myth about religious participation. Furthermore, the content and meaning of non-associational forms of religious participation has received little attention.

It has been demonstrated that neglect in research of religious behavior and social participation of the elderly is reflected in the lack of attention to this social-psychological aspect of life in professional gerontology meetings and in the major aging publications.

In addition to the policy implications identified, there are substantive issues that suggest research directions. First, it is clear that the measures used in religious research need to be critically evaluated for their reliability, validity, period effect, and relevancy for use with the elderly (particularly the frail elderly, 80 years of age and older). Variables such as sex, race, personal living situation, health, and social bonds need to be employed to help explain differences in religious behavior.

Finally, new measures and methodology, such as the life review, need to be developed and employed to relate religious behavior and practice in other stages of the life cycle to the current retirement stage. Many of the assumptions about the meaning and function of religion in late life will be challenged by new methodological approaches, and hopefully, a better understanding of the importance of religion to the elderly will no longer be a myth but a new reality.

REFERENCES

Albrecht, Ruth. The meaning of religion to the older person. In Denton L. Scudler (Ed.), *Organized religion and the older person.* Gainesville: University of Florida Press, 1958.

Bahr, Howard M. Aging and religious disaffiliation. *Social Forces,* 1970, *49,* 59-71.

Binstock, Robert H., & Shanas, Ethel (Eds.). *Handbook of aging and the social sciences.* New York: Van Nostrand, 1976.

Blazer, Dan, & Palmore, Erdman. Religion and aging in a longitudinal panel. *The Gerontologist,* 1976, *16,* 82-85.

Butler, Robert N., & Lewis, Myrna. *Aging and mental health.* St. Louis: C.V. Mosby, 1977.

Cavan, R.S., Burgess, E.W., Havighurst, R.J., & Goldhamer, N. *Personal adjustment to old age.* Chicago: Science Research Associates, 1949.

Cook, Thomas C., Jr. *The religious sector explores its mission in aging.* Final report on Administration on Aging grant number 93-HD-57390/4-03, Athens, Georgia: National Interfaith Coalition on Aging, 1976.

Cumming, Elaine, & Henry, William E. *Growing old.* New York: Basic Books, 1961.

Dumazedier, Joffre. *Sociology of leisure.* New York: Free Press, 1974.

Feifel, Herman. Religious conviction and fear of death among the healthy and the terminally ill. *Journal for the Scientific Study of Religion,* 1964, *13,* 353-360.

Fukuyama, Yoshio. The major dimensions of church membership. *Review of religious research,* 1961, *2,* 154-161.

Goody, Jack. Aging in non-industrial societies. In Robert Binstock and Ethel Shanas (Eds.), *Handbook of aging and the social sciences.* New York: Van Nostrand, 1976.

Hall, G.S. *Senescence, the second half of life.* New York: Appleton, 1922.

Harris, Louis and Associates. *The myth and reality of aging in America.* Washington, D.C.: National Council on the Aging, 1975.

Heenan, E.R. Aging in religious life. *Review of Religious Research,* 1968, *27,* 1120-1127.

Hendricks, Jon, & Hendricks, C. David. *Aging in mass society: Myths and realities.* Cambridge, Massachusetts: Winthrop Press, 1977.

Kalish, Richard A. Death and dying in social context. In Robert Binstock & Ethel Shanas (Eds.), *Handbook of aging and the social sciences.* New York: Van Nostrand, 1976.

Kimmel, Douglas. *Adulthood and aging.* New York: John Wiley, 1974.

Lowenthal, Marjorie Fiske, & Robinson, Betsy. Social networks and isolation. In Robert Binstock & Ethel Shanas (Eds.), *Handbook of aging and the social sciences.* New York: Van Nostrand, 1976.

Maves, Paul B. Aging, religion, and the church. In Clark Tibbitts (Ed.),

Handbook of social gerontology. Chicago: University of Chicago Press, 1960.

Moberg, David O. Religiosity in old age. In Bernice L. Neugarten (Ed.), *Middle age and aging.* Chicago: University of Chicago Press, 1968.

Moberg, David O. Religion in the later years. In Adeline Hoffman (Ed.), *The daily needs and interests of older people.* Springfield, Illinois: Charles C Thomas, 1970.

Moberg, David O. Needs felt by the clergy for ministries to the aging. *The Gerontologist,* 1975, *15,* 170-175.

Neugarten, Bernice (Ed.). *Middle age and aging.* Chicago: University of Chicago Press, 1968.

Orbach, Harold L. Aging and religion. *Geriatrics,* 1961, *16,* 530-540.

O'Reilly, C.T. Religious practice and personal adjustment of older people. *Sociology and Social Research,* 1957, *43,* 119-121.

Palmore, Erdman. Sociological aspects of aging. In Ewald Busse and Eric Pfeiffer (Eds.), *Behavior and adapatation in late life.* Boston: Little, Brown, 1969.

Palmore, Erdman. *Normal aging I.* Durham: Duke University Press, 1970.

Palmore, Erdman. *Normal aging II.* Durham: Duke University Press, 1974.

Payne, Barbara Pittard. The meaning and measurement of commitment to the church. Georgia State University, unpublished manuscript, 1965.

Payne, Barbara Pittard. Voluntary associations of the elderly. A paper presented to the annual meeting of the Society on the Study of Social Problems, New York City, 1973.

Payne, Barbara Pittard. Age differences in the meaning of leisure activities. A paper presented to the annual meeting of the Gerontological Society, Miami Beach, 1973.

Payne, Barbara Pittard. Religious life review. Georgia State University, unpublished field notes, 1977.

Payne, Barbara Pittard, & Whittington, Frank. Older women: An examination of popular stereotypes and research evidence. *Social Problems,* 1976, *23,* 488-504.

Payne, Raymond, Payne, Barbara Pittard, & Reddy, Richard D. Social background and role determinants of individual participation in organized voluntary action. *Voluntary action research.* Boston: D.C. Heath, 1972.

Riley, Matilda White, & Foner, Anne. *Aging and society: An inventory of research findings.* New York: Russell Sage Foundation, 1968.

Schuyler, Joseph. Religious observance differentials by age and sex in Northern parish. *American Catholic Sociological Review,* 1959, *20,* 124-131.

Starbuck, Ed. *The psychology of religion.* New York: Walter Scott, 1911.

Stark, R. Age and faith: A changing outlook at an old process. *Sociological Analysis,* 1968, *29,* 1-10.

Swenson, Wendell M. Attitudes toward death in an aging population. *Journal of Gerontology,* 1961, *16,* 49-52.

Taietz, A., & Larson, B. Social participation and old age. *Rural Sociology,* 1956,

21, 229-238.

Tibbitts, Clark (Ed.). *Handbook of social gerontology*. Chicago: University of Chicago Press, 1960.

U.S. Bureau of the Census. *Population reports*. Washington, D.C.: 1958.

Wingrove, C. Ray, & Alston, J.P. Age, aging, and church attendance. *The Gerontologist*, 1971, *11*, 356-358.

Woodruff, Diana S., & Birren, James E. *Aging: Scientific perspectives and social issues*. New York: Van Nostrand, 1975.

SCRIPTURAL INDEX

One possible reference to Apocryphal writings in Mother Bernadette deLourdes' chapter may be wrongfully labeled Ecclesiastes and possibly belongs to Ecclesiasticus. We have decided to leave it in the text as is. Rabbi Meier has one reference from the Old Testament scriptures and many from the Talmud, which he identifies. These are not included in this listing, but can be found in pages 161-168.

INDEX